Tutoring Writing
A Practical Guide for Conferences

DONALD A. McANDREW and THOMAS J. REIGSTAD

Foreword by Wendy Bishop

Boynton/Cook Publishers
HEINEMANN
Portsmouth, NH

This book is dedicated to the four McAndrew Ms:
Molly, Matt, Meg, and Marge,

and to the Reigstad clan: Leif, Lucas, and Maryanne.
Thanks for putting up with all the craziness.

Boynton/Cook Publishers, Inc.
A subsidiary of Reed Elsevier Inc.
361 Hanover Street
Portsmouth, NH 03801–3912
www.boyntoncook.com

Offices and agents throughout the world

Library of Congress Cataloging-in-Publication Data
McAndrew, Donald A.
    Tutoring writing : a practical guide for conferences / Donald A. McAndrew and Thomas J. Reigstad ; foreword by Wendy Bishop.
        p. cm.
    Includes bibliographical references.
        ISBN 0-86709-518-0 (alk. paper)
    1. English language—Rhetoric—Study and teaching. 2. Report writing—Study and teaching (Higher). 3. Tutors and tutoring. I. Reigstad, Thomas J. II. Title.
        PE1404 .M385 2001
        808'.042'071—dc21

                                                                        2001003812

Consulting editor: James Strickland
Editor: Lisa Luedeke
Production service: Melissa L. Inglis
Production coordination: Vicki Kasabian
Cover design: Joni Doherty
Manufacturing: Steve Bernier

Printed in the United States of America on acid-free paper
09 08 07 06   VP 6 7 8 9 10

Contents

Acknowledgments

We would like to thank Charles R. Cooper, who got us started as tutors at the Writing Place, SUNY/Buffalo. We would also like to thank our friend Jim Strickland, who encouraged us to undertake this project and who made a fine model author and kind editor. Don would like to thank Trocaire College for allowing him to create a writing center and tutor-training program from the ground up. Tom would like to thank Donald Murray for his inspiration in how to tutor writers with wisdom and understanding.

Foreword

What Tutoring Writing Should Be

Welcome to the "little book" that grew. When I first read *Tutoring Writing*'s precursor, I had recently left a summer classroom in Pennsylvania, a course "Teaching College Writing," taught by Don McAndrew, and returned to the University of Alaska where I was developing a new writing center. Had I ever done this before? No. Was I confident that I could? Yes. Not only had I studied writing theory and practice under the most engaged of writing teachers, but I had also been introduced to Thomas A. Reigstad and Donald M. McAndrew's NCTE monograph "Training Tutors for Writing Conferences." That little book with the white and red cover had been waved under my nose the summer of 1985 by Don's colleague, and my eventual dissertation committee member, Patrick Hartwell. Pat, who was gaining recognition for his now well-known essay "Grammar, Grammars, and the Teaching of Grammar," reveled in calling the tutoring book *little* but he did it with proud, impish good humor. He knew these authors would provide all I'd need to set up my center. And they did.

In fact, I didn't know then that I'd continue to find their theoretical review and practical suggestions about tutoring writing honorably supporting my own teaching essays, guiding my writing center research, and echoing through section after section of my course syllabi over the next decade and beyond. Discussions of HOCs and LOCs—terms coined by these authors—eased countless classroom conversations because the language of higher order concerns and lower order concerns made so much sense to my students and to me, facilitating our talk, demystifying writing (see Chapter 6 in this book). And that's the skill of these author educators: They help us make sense of what we're doing. For instance, I knew about and practiced freewriting but it was meditation on the McAndrew and Reigstad discussion of *focused freewriting* (see Chapter 5 in this book) that allowed me to create sequences of classroom writing inventions that worked their way into several published textbooks on the teaching of creative writing.

Of the many books on my teaching bookshelf, I never loaned out my monograph. I always kept it at hand. In fact, it's still there while other loaned books have gone the way of loaned books. And today it returns to me amplified, enlarged, and enriched, for that monograph has turned into *Tutoring Writing*, a more experienced and even wiser version of that instrumental youngster.

Reading this book I return to my teaching roots, which are firm and deep. I can trace the influence of Reigstad and McAndrew as this book traces the work of master tutors on the tutoring profession through the histories of exemplary educators like Donald Murray, Roger Garrison, Donald Graves, Muriel Harris, Walker Gibson, Nancie Atwell, Peter Elbow, and Thomas Newkirk. As a fundamental reference work and introduction, *Tutoring Writing* is clear *and* it is erudite. It practices what it preaches. It's a coach, upbeat and fun to read. It's a listener to my tutoring questions. It's a teacher of effective practices.

I liked the voice of Tom and Don, the teachers in the monograph: they wanted me to succeed (I did, the center grew and flourished). In fact, I can't remember those days without recalling the number of times the authors' notion of having a "priority of concerns" helped me sit down and figure out the same as a writing center director, as a tutor educator, as a tutor. I think of the copies of the many tutoring questions they provided which I photocopied and enlarged and pinned to the tutors' bulletin board and handed out to students to use as they tutored each other, in classes, as peer tutors.

I like even more the voices of the teachers I (re)meet today in *Tutoring Writing* because they are no longer constrained by the page limits of that earlier volume. Don McAndrew and Tom Reigstad have had another decade, and then some, to study and support their work. And they've been working hard all that time.

Again, clarity, practicality, good and generous advice, and training savvy prevail, grounded in theory and practice. Again, I nod along:

> Writers, like other human beings, see through false praise—but writers are particularly sensitive and suspicious when tutors give them a steady stream of positive comments about their work. Writers need honest feedback, not empty flattery. One of Nancie Atwell's (1998) guidelines for conducting one-to-one conferences is "avoid generalized praise."
>
> Don't misunderstand: Positive stroking is good. But tutors should not use praise to sugarcoat the truth. (17)

The blend of illustration, advice, research, experience, and understanding of this sort is a hallmark of the book you are about to read.

You'll find particularly timely material about tutoring in different places (Chapter 7), tutoring different people (Chapter 8) and lessons from the masters (Chapter 9). These chapters remind readers that the one-to-one conference between teacher and student, tutor and client, and classmate and peer has revolutionized the way we think about learning to write. Writers talk to other writers, at home, at work, in school. Writers have needs that are the same and different; needs that are about writing processes in general but about their own writing process in particular. Peer tutoring is now the cornerstone of the writing world we live in as compositionists and this book supports all aspects of that world, above all, the needs of the new tutor and the tutor educator.

Review the theory—you'll find it sound and well organized. Take the course—it works. I took it and taught it and will do so again. Try the "How I Write" essay for yourself. Discover. Practice. This book helps you write and talk about writing with your students, peers, clients, your world of writers. The authors don't sugarcoat the truth. They praise what works. They're rightly suspicious about what goes under the guise of good tutoring but clearly isn't. They'll do their best to steer you straight. Best of all, they like what they do as tutor educators. I have no doubt that their advice will help you create a clean, well-lighted tutoring moment.

After reading *Tutoring Writing*, my bumper sticker (see Chapter 5) says "Honk If You Talked Good Writing Talk Today." With the help of *Tutoring Writing*, it happens.

WENDY BISHOP

Introduction

Introduction as History

In 1976, we were both doctoral students at the State University of New York at Buffalo. To celebrate the opening of the Writing Place, the writing center at SUNY/Buffalo, Charles R. Cooper, then a faculty member, organized a symposium on tutoring writing in writing centers. He invited Mary Croft of the University of Wisconsin/Stevens Point and Robert Gundlach of Northwestern University to be the featured speakers. It was this symposium that sparked our interest in tutoring writing. After that first spark, we each tutored at the Writing Place.

Then we went different ways. Tom went to the SUNY College at Buffalo, where he trained tutors for the writing center, trained secondary English teachers, and taught composition and literature courses. Don went to Trocaire College, a private two-year college in Buffalo, where he acted as director of developmental skills, created a writing center, and taught composition and literature. Don received a federal Vocational Education Act grant to develop the writing center, and he hired Tom as a consultant. From that collaboration came the 1984 monograph *Training Tutors for Writing Conferences*, part of the National Council of Teachers of English "Theory and Research into Practice" (TRIP) series. The monograph won the Best Publication for Writing Center Practice in 1985 from the National Writing Centers Association.

Don then moved to Indiana University of Pennsylvania to teach in the doctoral program in rhetoric and linguistics, which trains college composition teachers, and the English education program, which trains secondary English teachers. He also began to consult with elementary, secondary, and college teachers in six states about improving the teaching of literacy, and to speak to PTAs and parent groups about the role of parents and homes in children's literacy development.

Tom continued his work with writing centers and teacher education, and worked part time as a feature writer and editor for the Buffalo *Courier-Express*. He also began to consult with business and industry about improving the writing skills of workers and managers, and continued to consult with area school districts about improving the teaching of writing in secondary schools.

Fifteen years after the publication of *Training Tutors for Writing Conferences*, James Strickland, a long time friend and consulting editor for this project, approached us about redoing the monograph to reflect both the developments that had been made in theory and research in composition studies since its original publication, and the wider audiences we had been working with—parents in the home and writers in business and industry. From that stimulus came this book.

Introduction as Theory

Since 1984, teaching writing has blossomed into a major scholarly field, attracting researchers from across the disciplines, developing theories about written language and its teaching, and leading to substantial changes in the classroom practices of teaching writing at all levels of schooling. It seemed to us that the time was ripe to update our discussion of teaching writing through one-to-one tutorials.

In our own teaching and consulting work we had been talking about tutoring writing in new ways, introducing new theoretical and research support, new understandings of the processes of tutoring, and new discussions of the people and places where tutoring occurs. This book lays out those new discussions about tutoring writing.

Chapter 1 reviews the major theoretical support for tutoring writing: social constructionism, reader response literary theory, theories of talk and writing, collaborative learning, and feminism. Chapter 2 lays out the research support for one-to-one tutoring of writers, whether that support comes from research on peer response groups, conferencing one-to-one with the teacher, or tutoring itself.

To help readers identify situations that seem to be one-to-one tutoring but that are in fact something different and less effective, Chapter 3 describes what tutoring is *not*, including the interactions of editor and journalist and those of therapist and client. Chapter 4 describes what tutoring actually *is* by explaining the writing process and the tutoring process. Chapter 5 talks about how to tutor writers who have either no draft or only a partial draft, and Chapter 6 discusses how to tutor writers in the most common situation, where they have a complete draft. Chapters 4, 5, and 6 describe many strategies that tutors can use to help writers improve both their drafts and the writing process that leads to them. The chapters also include examples of tutorials of various types that tutors can use as models.

Chapter 7 looks at three tutoring venues that are not usually mentioned in discussions of tutoring, which typically focus on writing centers and classrooms: in writing across the curriculum

programs in schools and colleges, on the job in business and industry, and at home. Chapter 8 examines how the tutorial situation is
affected by different kinds of people (and the differences between
them)—not just the writing center visitors and classroom students
who are typically discussed—including high ability writers, gender
difference between tutor and writer, multicultural and ESL (English
as a second language) tutors and writers, learning disabled and special education tutors and writers, and tutors and writers with different learning styles and personalities.

Chapter 9 pulls all the previous discussion together by showing
eight master tutors at work—Donald Murray, Peter Elbow, Muriel
Harris, Thomas Newkirk, Donald Graves, Nancie Atwell, Roger
Garrison, and Walker Gibson. Chapter 10 describes using electronic
technology (telephone, fax, e-mail, the World Wide Web, and online
writing labs) for tutoring. And Chapter 11 outlines a tutor-training
course that can be offered for as long as a semester or for just a few days.

Chapter One

Theories Underpinning Tutoring Writing

Tutoring writing stands on firm theoretical ground, connecting with major theoretical developments across disciplines during the past twenty-five years. The theory of tutoring suggests a powerful way to help a writer grow in skill and confidence and also supplies tutors with direction in their practice since these theories have direct implications for the practice of tutoring. Five major theoretical strands underpin tutoring: social constructionist theory, reader response literary theories, theories of talk and writing, collaborative learning, and feminism.

Social Constructionism

Social constructionist theory has been influential across many disciplines, affecting both their central tenets and their research methodology. In composition theory, social constructionist theory was introduced through the work of Kenneth Bruffee in composition studies, Mikial Bakhtin in literary theory, and Lev Vygotsky in psycholinguistics.

Social constructionists emphasize that language is "social," a phenomenon of societies, both created by them and serving them. Language exists at a social level among its users, connecting self with others through a web or net of shared ideas. Even when a writer might seem to be writing alone, she is still connected to others because she thinks of the audience to whom she writes, and she thinks of what she has read, heard, said, and written previously. She is always a part of society, just as language itself is, so writing is primarily a social act. As Bruffee (1986) says, "We use language primarily to join communities we do not yet belong to and to cement our membership in communities we already belong to" (784).

Social constructionists also remind us that language and culture are a construction of humans as they enter into relatedness through language. Humans construct meaning, communication, and knowledge, thereby constructing their world and themselves. We create our personal understandings by using language; others share our understandings by reading or listening to the language we use. This sharing of individual perspectives is the dialogue that creates us and our world. Our participation in the dialogue expresses, allows, and creates our self and our society simultaneously as we in turn are created by that society and its language. Bakhtin (1981) summarizes nicely, explaining that every utterance "exists in other people's mouths, in other people's contexts, serving other people's intentions" (91). From this "other people" or social orientation comes the power and the necessity of dialogue as the source of language, knowledge, and culture.

Language and learning occur through interaction with society. Vygotsky (1978) explains that students have an "actual developmental level" in their language and literacy development, the level at which they can work without assistance. But they also have a "level of potential development"—the level at which they could work if they had the help of a teacher or an able peer coaching them to move beyond what they can currently do. So, for Vygotsky, "Human learning presupposes a specific social nature and a process by which children grow into the intellectual life of those around them" (88). In this process, the teacher is a more experienced writer or language user who asks questions and supports students to help them progress.

Tutoring and other forms of one-to-one instruction directly demonstrate the social nature of language, literacy, and learning. The tutor acts as a coach, enabling the writer to take a step forward in writing generally and in this draft specifically. What we see when we watch a tutoring session is a social interaction that's focused on literacy and learning, a dialogue between the more experienced tutor and the less experienced student writer that takes place in the wider context of language and culture. The writer will reconstruct her understanding of the current draft and of writing as a direct result of the dialogue. Social construction, dialogue, literacy, and learning all interweave during a tutoring session, exemplifying and reinforcing the social constructionist theory that's at the heart of the tutor/writer interaction.

Reader Response Literary Theories

Reader response literary theories include two related theories that underpin the power and process of tutoring writing—David Bleich's *subjective criticism* and Louise Rosenblatt's *transactional criticism*. Reader response theories rose as a reaction against the New Criticism of the 1940s–60s, which held that the fixed meaning of a literary work is in the text and accessible to the reader through careful analysis.

Subjective criticism, the more radical of the two theories, gives prominence to the reader over the text, arguing that the text is merely a culturally agreed upon pattern of ink symbols on paper. The real meaning—the real literature, as it were—is in the reader's response to those symbols. Meaning is, therefore, made by the reader, not by the text; reading is the act of interpretation based on the reader's previous experiences, not just the act of finding or collecting from the text. The reader shares her responses through talk and writing with the larger community of readers, and this sharing enriches the readers' meaning-making. Bleich (1975) believes that readers respond to a work, consider each other's responses through talk and writing, and build an enriched understanding of the work and its literary merit. The act of reading and literature's effect on the reader are simultaneously subjective and communal, since a reader's interpretation is the result of both her individual experiences and the sociocultural context of those experiences, including the current act of reading-interpreting.

Rosenblatt's (1978) transactional criticism is less radical than Bleich's subjectivist stance because it allows a much larger place for the text in understanding how a work of literature is read. She states, "What each reader makes of the text is, indeed, *for him* the poem . . . what he himself experiences in relation to the text is—again let us underline—*for him*, the work" (105). But she adds, differing from Bleich, that the reader is not outside the control of the text and that the text structures, directs, and provides new material. The reader creates the meaning or interpretation by conducting a transaction with the text, by thinking the thoughts of another—the writer—in regard to both material and structure. The text enables the reader to create the new, to reformulate based on previous experiences and on the material and directions of the text. The text and the reader, then, act upon on each other, forming the meaning together. Both text and reader are active.

In tutoring writing, text, reader, and tutor are active. The writer's draft sits between the tutor and the writer, all three in a context of interaction. The tutor creates an interpretation of the draft and shares it. The writer does the same. The draft-as-text structures, directs, and supplies new material. Tutoring writing—where reader, writer, text, and context are all for a moment together and visible—demonstrates reader response theories at work in the world.

Talk and Writing

Knowing the power of oral language as a way to learn in general, and to learn writing specifically, is another theoretical ground for tutoring. Douglas Barnes (1990) calls for teachers to encourage students to talk more in class because students "have already taken possession of complex ways of making sense of the world . . . for the social and cognitive skills they have developed in various contexts in and out of school provide their most valuable resources as learners" (54). Students are far more experienced as talkers than as readers or writers, and Barnes argues for mobilizing that experience to serve learning and literacy. He sees "exploratory talk"—an informal, tentative talking it over—as beneficial for learning, especially for learning writing. In tutoring writing, talk is both the writer's internal process of reflective dialogue and an external act in which the writer actively engages with tutor, teacher, or peers in an attempt to clarify textual meaning. Barnes believes that talk "enables students to represent to themselves what they currently understand and then if necessary criticize and change it" (50).

Wendy Bishop (1992) sees talk as being central to the whole process of writing: "Writers compose through inner speech while talking, by speaking aloud at the word processor, when discussing a work-in-progress, or as they share ideas during conferences in writing centers and classrooms" (6).

The hum of talk that's an almost constant part of composing is rarely recognized and discussed. Donald Rubin and William Dodd (1987) see this invisibility as being unfortunate, because not recognizing that talk is part of the writing process makes teachers and students believe that writing is learned by writing alone. In reality, talk allows writers to bounce their ideas off an audience, which requires them to practice rhetorical skills as they adjust the ideas to the audience, and they thus develop the analytical and critical skills that are essential to drafting and revising.

Tutoring writing mobilizes talk in the service of improving writing competencies. In one important way, tutoring is talk, two people discussing the process that's underway. Early in the process, tutor and writer might talk about a focus for the unstarted draft, searching the writer's life for issues or experiences to write about. As the process moves along, talk can be a number of things: developing ideas or sections of the draft, developing rhetorical constraints, answers to open-ended questions from the tutor, praise of well-crafted phrases and sentences, role-playing audiences, or simply reading the draft aloud. Whatever it consists of and whenever it takes place, talk is the substance of tutoring.

The talk that's involved in tutoring also affects the relationship between the tutor and the writer. A writer who spends time talking to a tutor cannot help but understand that the tutor cares about her and her growth as a writer. Talk is the cement of social relationships in and out of school. When talk is mobilized in tutoring, the relationship between tutor and writer develops. Not only does the connection between them grow, but the writer sees that writing isn't necessarily solitary and the tutor sees that talking about writing makes her own understanding of it grow. Talk about writing pays both writer and tutor with growth in writing and personal relationships. Perhaps that is why those who use tutoring report that it is just plain enjoyable.

Collaborative Learning

Kenneth Bruffee (1973) sees the big picture of *collaborative learning*, describing it as part of a wider movement that includes the development of more democratic and participatory political structures and nonauthoritarian, shared decision making in nations and organizations. Collaborative learning organizes people not just to work together on common projects, but, more importantly, to engage in a process of intellectual, social, and personal negotiation that leads to collective decision making. Collaborative learning by its nature opposes totalitarianism and alienation and encourages communitarianism and connectedness.

Andrea Lunsford and Lisa Ede (1986) see collaborative learning as demonstrating how knowledge is constructed in most social and work communities. For Frank Smith (1988), all learning is fundamentally collaborative, requiring two people: one who is a member of the club and one who wants to be. They work together with trust in each other and confidence in themselves, and learning happens incidentally to their focus on collaboration; for example, the child learns to speak not as a direct result of instruction but as an indirect result of collaborating with adults and other children to accomplish things.

According to Anne Gere (1987), collaborative learning in education and classrooms ameliorates the alienation of society and its schools, which are full of competitive egocentrism, by reorienting writers toward their readers in a way that helps them comprehend the connective nature of composing for readers. Gere observes that those involved in collaborative learning exhibit certain educationally advantageous characteristics: They challenge one another with questions, use the evidence and information available to them, develop relationships among issues, and evaluate their thinking. Specifically for writing, Gere sees collaborative learning as "the process of working together [which] enables writers to use language as a means of becoming competent in the discourse of a given community" (75).

Tutoring writing is a type of collaborative learning. The tutor and the writer are connected as they question, propose, and evaluate both the draft and their interaction. The writer gets the experience of having a real reader and of seeing reactions to her words, and she asks questions and responds to prompts. The tutor watches a draft develop, probing and supporting as the writer makes and evaluates decisions. Both writer and tutor grow as writers because they collaborate on the process and the product of writing.

Feminism

Feminist theory attempts to explain where the spirit of collaboration arises and why it works. Feminism also gives us insights into why talk and dialogue, reader response, and social construction are important in tutoring. Carol Gilligan (1982) charted a model of women's psychological and moral development that placed relationships and caring for others at the center, opposing the assertive individualism and competitive self-centeredness of the traditional classroom. Mary Belenky et al. (1986) expanded our understanding of human cognitive development. As opposed to the traditional view that knowledge and knowing are abstract, objective, and individual, they describe a form of cognitive development that relies on "connected knowing" across experiences and relationships, which they conclude women exhibit more often than men do. In this view, the classroom is a place of interaction between not just teacher and student but also student and student. Talk and authentic discussion, not teacher-led questioning, is the rule, and the teacher's and students' experiences with and responses to text become the central issue.

Feminist theories of teaching and learning synthesized the theories and recommendations of social constructionism, reader response, talk and writing, and collaborative learning into a whole that showed a new understanding of how we learn and develop literacy, of the relationship between teacher and students, and of who is actually the teacher as peers share knowledge and facilitate each other's learning. Frances Maher and Mary Kay Thompson Tetreault (1994) examined teachers' and students' actions in classrooms across the country and identified three distinct aspects of feminist teaching. First, it redefines subject mastery as seeking knowledge on personal terms and in concert with others, which immerses students in a community of knowers who develop increasingly complex expressions of their understanding. Second, it awakens students' voices, encouraging and supporting them in expressing their responses and life experiences. Classroom activity often consists of students bringing their own questions and perspectives to the issues, shaping their own evolving, knowing voices in the process. Third, it establishes a new authority in the classroom: Students are responsible for their own learning because the learning is grounded in their life experiences. Classroom authority results from the mixture of self and community, response and sharing, and narrative and connection that takes place in the ongoing conversation of a learning community.

One-to-one writing tutoring might be considered a form of feminist teaching: It honors relationships and caring as tutor and writer work together toward a common goal. The student grows as a writer in each session, developing mastery on personal terms by talking with the tutor about the process and product that's at the center. The student develops her voice as a writer and learner as the tutor encourages and supports her questions, responses, and perspectives about the current draft, the process that is producing it, and the writer's ongoing literacy growth. Authority for the piece of writing and the tutoring session lies in the negotiation and consensus that writer and tutor develop through their conversation.

Chapter Two

Research Supporting Tutoring Writing

This chapter further describes the grounds for tutoring writing, reviewing the research that has been done on tutoring and conferencing (a form of tutoring in which the tutor is a teacher rather than a peer) and discussing groups in which multiple peers respond to the writer's developing draft.

Research is used here to mean only empirical studies, whether quantitative/statistical or qualitative/naturalistic. The term *research* is used less strictly across the literature on tutoring, conferencing, and peer groups, so the "research ground" for tutoring is often built on theoretical discussions or pedagogical recommendations rather than on actual research. The research included in this chapter is work that studied tutoring, conferencing, or peer groups to learn about their effectiveness, not simply to discuss them. We decided to be strict in our use of the term because we were curious about what strict research support for tutoring writing looked like.

We present this research support by identifying particular studies and discussing the conclusions they support. This strikes us as being the most useful approach for those who would train writing tutors. We have also assumed that those who train tutors need evidence that supports tutoring writing, not studies that question tutoring or one of its features. Thus, we say little about those studies. We believe that someone who is preparing to train writing tutors needs to know what research support he has; indeed, the research overwhelmingly supports tutoring writing.

Research on Peer Response Groups

Research on the effectiveness of peer groups as a form of tutoring is abundant. Researchers across grades have tried to establish peer response or peer editing groups as an alternative to the traditional teacher-centered lecture that has dominated most writing and literacy classrooms (Toth 1997; McManus and Kirby 1988; Shannon 1983; Lagana 1972).

Researchers have specifically characterized the growth that peer groups foster, concluding that students in peer groups do the following:

- Develop audience awareness (Shannon 1983; Ziv 1983; Beaven 1977).

- Develop revision abilities, risk-taking creativity, and interpersonal skills (Beaven 1977).

- Increase their ability to deal with higher order concerns such as clarity of focus and development, doing much more than just editing the surface structure of the pieces (Bruffee 1978).

- Show an implicit grasp of the nature of academic writing and accurately distinguish between major and minor writing problems (Danis 1980).

- Show personal involvement, self-initiated learning, and self-evaluation (Hawkins 1976).

- Exercise their judgment and are able to explain things to each other in more understandable language than that used by the professor (Rizzo 1975).

- Encourage and question each other and demonstrate ownership of their pieces (Freedman 1987).

Some researchers have looked at the talk in peer groups in order to better understand how the groups foster growth in writing abilities, concluding that peer groups do the following:

- Develop their own metalanguage about writing that allows them to discuss writing processes and products in ways that teacher-supplied language rarely does (Hamilton-Wieler 1990).

- Develop a language of negotiation that is rich with both phatic-hedged forms and directives for revisions (Drechsel 1989).

- Often focus on metaresponse—discussion of the assignment, class context, and group procedures (Benesch 1985).

- Often focus on the content of the writing and its communicative value even when the teacher is not present (Gere and Abbott 1985).

- Use group talk to provide suggestions that writers used to improve their papers (Gere 1982).
- Use increasingly more group talk over time as writers think more carefully about their papers (David 1985).

Researchers have taken a wider focus and attempted to connect peer response groups to theoretical changes in composition studies, especially the paradigmatic change from focusing on writing processes rather than on written products (DiPardo and Freedman 1988). Others have looked at group interaction itself, finding that it varies with class environment and assignments: In some classes the interaction focuses on evaluating the quality of drafts, while in others it focuses on collaborating to develop ideas and content for the piece (Freedman 1987). George (1984) characterizes the best group interaction as being task-oriented, with all group members speaking and listening to each other. Kurth (1995) found leadership in groups to be situational, varying in accordance with who has the most to contribute. Zhu (1995) found that the best interaction can be expected from groups that are carefully trained, because the great variation in response groups calls for training and modeling by the teacher, as Hacker (1994) documented, and because such training produces writing with greater maturity and sophistication, as Gilliam (1995) described.

Research on Conferences

Using one-to-one conferences between teacher and student became a prominent writing instruction strategy in the 1970s. Early research found that conferences are as effective as the traditional lecture class (Kates 1977; Sutton 1975) and often lead to more positive attitudes toward writing and writing classes (Budz and Graber 1976; Tomlinson 1975). In attempting to explain their positive effects on writing skills and attitudes, researchers argued that the dialogic nature of the conference allows the writer to participate in the process of evaluating the piece (Freedman 1980) and that the writing conference provides a particularly effective setting for writers to critically reflect on their product and process (Freedman and Calfee 1984). Jacobs and Karliner (1977) noted that the process of reflection and evaluation was more prevalent in conferences rated high in effectiveness by participants than in those rated low. Scardamalia and Bereiter (1985) found that one result of the social interaction in conferences—reflection and evaluation—developed from a flexible, continuing focus on the individual writer's cognitive and linguistic knowledge and needs.

More-recent research has attempted to fine-tune what is a very complex instructional interaction. Researchers have demonstrated that the interaction in one-to-one conferences varies greatly depending on who is involved: The interaction is a unique product of *this* teacher and *this* student on *this* occasion (Sperling 1990; Ulichny and Watson-Gegeo 1989; Florio-Ruane 1986). In fact, writing conferences are difficult to generalize about because each student has different abilities, different goals for this piece and for learning about writing, and different views of his role as a student (Sperling 1991). But conferences exist across a spectrum, ranging from teacher-centered through collaborative to student-centered (Reigstad 1980).

Researchers have identified why conferences fail: Too often, the teacher dominates both time and agenda (Walker and Elias 1987) or focuses on surface mechanics at the expense of higher-order issues like development and organization (Freedman 1981; Freedman and Sperling 1985). Researchers have also identified why conferences succeed: The teacher creates a deliberative and critical conversational context (Sperling 1991); or patiently tolerates the hesitant, repetitious, awkward, staccato dialogue typical of conferences with writers (Newkirk 1995); or shifts the conference roles and processes to meet the student's cultural expectations in ways that range from the implicit and less-directive "suggestions" style of U.S. middle-class students to the authoritative and decisive "expectations" style of some African American (Delpit 1988) and ESL students (Patthey-Chavez and Ferris 1997).

Research on Tutoring

Empirical studies of tutoring can be divided into three categories: studies of peer tutoring in general; studies of tutoring literacy; and studies of tutoring writing itself. Direct research support for tutoring writing comes from all three.

Studies of Peer Tutoring in General

Research on peer tutoring in a variety of disciplines and at various age and grade levels supports five conclusions that have significant implications for tutoring writing. Martino (1994); Slavin (1991); Gautrey (1990); Benard (1990); Greenwood, Delquadri, and Hall (1989); Hedin (1987); Levin, Glass, and Meister (1984); and Cohen, Kulik, and Kulik (1982) found that

1. peer tutoring is generally effective in improving the skills and knowledge of the person who is tutored

2. peer tutoring is perhaps even more effective in improving the skills and knowledge of the tutor

3. peer tutoring improves the social development of those involved

4. peer tutors should be carefully trained

5. peer tutoring is cost-effective

Studies of Tutoring Literacy

Studies of tutoring as a method of teaching literacy are many, and they confirm the five conclusions about peer tutoring. These studies establish the overall effectiveness of tutoring literacy, add specific details to our understanding of tutoring literacy, and synthesize prior research about tutoring literacy.

Not surprisingly, given that elementary and middle schools are the predominant sites for teaching literacy in our culture, many studies of tutoring's effect on reading and writing abilities have been done on elementary students. From the studies conducted by Carli (1996); Judy et al. (1988); Mooney (1986); and Hahn and Smith (1983), it is fair to conclude that tutoring is an effective way to increase literacy skills, whether those skills are measured by standardized achievement or reading tests or by other methods, such as teacher observations or surveys of actual reading and writing.

Some studies detail finer aspects of tutoring literacy, concluding that it produces substantial gains in comprehension, the central issue in learning to read (Hall 1994; Perry 1991; Atherley 1989; Pickens and McNaughton 1988), and improves students' self-esteem (Hall 1994; Perry 1991; Ross 1972) and attitudes toward literacy and school (Thames and Reeves 1994; Leach 1987). These improvements affect students of all ages, from children in the primary grades through adults, and affect tutors and students equally (Morgan 1990; Annis 1983).

Finally, several researchers have synthesized or reviewed research to reach conclusions across studies. Barbara Wasik and Robert Slavin (1993) reviewed sixteen studies of five different tutoring models and concluded that tutoring causes substantial positive growth in literacy that lasts over time. The Canadian Teachers Federation (1991) reviewed thirteen studies and concluded that tutoring has beneficial effects, especially when there is a strong connection between reading and writing and when there is parental involvement. Martha Rekrut (1994), after reviewing studies from the previous twenty-five years, concluded that many elements of literacy, whether cognitive or affective, are amenable to tutoring; tutoring is effective for all age groups; and tutors should be trained in interpersonal, management, and content skills.

Studies on Tutoring Writing

Studies on tutoring writing are less numerous than those on peer tutoring and tutoring literacy, but are of great importance to establishing the research ground for improving writing skills through tutoring. The full research support for tutoring writing comes from the sum of the research on tutoring writing and tutoring literacy and peer tutoring along with less direct but important support from research on conferencing and peer groups.

Research support for tutoring writing again confirms the five conclusions of the research on peer tutoring. Tutoring writing is an effective way to develop writing skills in students from the early primary grades (Toth 1997; Meroney 1994; Tucker 1990) through the college years (Song and Richter 1997; Deming 1986; Smith 1975) and into adulthood (Gorman 1981). Tutoring also improves the quality of the written product (Smith 1975), the effectiveness of the writing process (Deming 1986), students' chances of passing the writing course they are taking (Song and Richter 1997), and students' grades in writing courses (Land 1987; MacDonald 1987) and scores on standardized writing tests (Meroney 1994). It is also effective at developing the affective domain related to growth in writing by improving writers' attitudes (Davis 1987; Smith 1975) and their perceptions of themselves as writers (Toth 1997). In addition, Smith and Smith (1988) found that tutoring writing improves grades in English 101 courses more effectively than traditional grammar instruction does, while Meroney (1994) and Jordan-Henley and Maid (1995) concluded that tutoring writing works well in a computerized learning environment.

Chapter Three

What Tutoring Writing Isn't

This chapter looks at tutoring by using Aristotle's method of arguing from opposites, exploring what the tutoring of writers is *not*. Although tutoring writing is one-to-one, it is unlike other one-to-one situations, and the writing tutor should not emulate those other situations. Tutoring writers is *not*

- patterned after the typical conference between a professional editor and a journalist
- giving false praise
- simply detecting and correcting errors
- adopting the cloak of therapist
- taking ownership away from the writer
- necessarily having all the answers
- responding too late

The Editor-Journalist Model

Over the, years well-intentioned writing teachers from Mina Shaughnessy (1977) to Charles Moran (1994) have promoted the editor-journalist relationship as an ideal that writing tutors ought to imitate. This model once served a useful purpose by encouraging writing teachers to transform traditional teacher-centered classrooms into more individualized, student-oriented workshop environments, but its value for writing tutors has been distorted and misrepresented.

The myth of the nurturing, caring editor working side-by-side with an author has been perpetuated and glamorized by stories about Maxwell Perkins, the legendary editor at Charles Scribner's Sons who worked with such authors as Ernest Hemingway, F. Scott Fitzgerald, Thomas Wolfe, and Marjorie Rawlings. At first glance, Perkins would seem to be the prototype for a perfect writing tutor. He adhered to a simple principle: "An editor does not add to a book. At best he serves as a handmaiden to an author" (Berg 1978). Perkins adjusted his mentoring style to fit the author. He often paid personal visits to Fitzgerald and Hemingway to discuss their drafts, and he spent a great deal of time with Wolfe. Most of Perkins' feedback to Rawlings was delivered through extensive correspondence.

Perkins is the exception rather than the rule; the typical editor-professional writer relationship is more of an "antimodel" for writing tutors.

Tom Reigstad worked as a copy editor at a daily newspaper in a large city. In two years on the job, he had only one direct conversation with a reporter about a story (and it was by phone, not face-to-face) because such contact would have violated the unofficial pecking order of the newsroom. If copy editors had questions about a story, they went through a chain of command: to the chief copy editor, who went to the city editor, who might then phone the reporter. Copy editors and reporters rarely consulted with each other about pieces of writing.

Maryanne Reigstad and Meghan McAndrew attest to the surprisingly antagonistic nature of the editor-writer relationship in journalism. In reminiscing about her seven years as a professional journalist, Reigstad (1990) identifies just one editor who behaved as a "teacher"; who was "adept at working with writers to let them see for themselves what information was lacking, and how the piece could become better." Reigstad mostly encountered editors who had their own agendas: When they assigned a story, they had a preconceived notion of what it would be like and did not welcome a surprising fact or twist if the reporter collected data that did not fit that notion. McAndrew's three years as a newspaper reporter also confirm that the editor-writer model is not a desirable one for writing tutors to follow. When time was not an issue, her editor would talk about a piece he had assigned her, or about other pieces she had written that he thought were particularly effective, or even about writing in general. But when the time crunch was on, as it frequently is in newspaper work, he took control of the process and product. McAndrew found more sympathetic readers in and got more down-to-earth advice from other reporters, with whom she frequently discussed pieces.

Donald Murray helps shatter the myth that the bond between editors and reporters is like the one between tutors and students. Murray, a writing teacher, former journalist, and pioneer in the field of tutoring writers, provides many firsthand accounts that suggest that real-life, editor-journalist conferences are more adversarial than collegial.

Some of Murray's most revealing anecdotes come from his days as a staff member at *Time* magazine. He admits that he "didn't learn much about writing from the *Time* editor who made a glider out of one of my stories and tossed it out the twenty-eighth story window" (1985). He also expresses disgust over editors' stylistic changes: "When I was on *Time* I sometimes felt that the senior editors (senior rewriters) would choose the metaphor over the story. It was not a good way to go" (1983). Murray calls his tenure at *Time* "a disaster. I resisted editing. I found that most editors were absolutist in what they had to say. They were curt and authoritarian . . . they were a burden that I had to put up with to get ahead in the profession . . . I don't think that they were a model for teaching" (1979a).

Murray (1961) writes about submitting a 5,300-word article to the *Saturday Evening Post* and receiving a letter of criticism from the editor that was 3,750 words long. He and the editor eventually met and went over the article word by word. The editor offered to rewrite it, an offer that Murray declined.

Among Murray's chief criticisms of editors is that they don't listen to writers and don't invite quality work. Like Reigstad, Murray finds editors to be overly rigid, expecting writers to jump through hoops of conventional prose and formulas. He says that "the usual city room climate outlaws risk. . . . That climate can be reversed if the editor stops behaving as top sergeant, treating reporters as troops on latrine duty, and makes writers colleagues" (1989).

In the last fifteen years newspapers have attempted to repair the distrust between editors and writers by hiring consultants to serve as writing coaches, which has greatly improved both journalistic writing and the relationships between editors and writers. Coaching journalists has become a kind of cottage industry, with a newsletter, "Coaches' Corner," and a book, *Coaching Writers* (Clark and Fry 1992), targeted to newspaper writing coaches. But until such coaching achieves more widespread change in journalistic practices, the traditional newspaper editor-writer relationship will be of limited use as a model for writing tutors, perhaps even functioning as an antimodel, a modus operandi to be avoided—despite the persistent myth in popular and education-related literature that professional editors and writers collaborate in a pervasive spirit of goodwill.

Cheerleading

Writers, like other human beings, see through false praise—but writers are particularly sensitive and suspicious when tutors give them a steady stream of positive comments about their work. Writers need honest feedback, not empty flattery. One of Nancie Atwell's (1998) guidelines for conducting one-to-one conferences is "avoid generalized praise."

Don't misunderstand: Positive stroking is good. But tutors should not use praise to sugarcoat the truth. Atwell goes on to suggest how tutors can compliment writers when it is warranted:

> Praise by paying attention to the writer. Praise by becoming involved in the writing. Praise by congratulating writers who solve problems by dint of hard work. Praise by acknowledging writers who try something new. Praise by describing the effects of specific techniques on you as a reader. (225)

The distinction between genuine and false praise is an important one for tutors to keep in mind.

Donald Murray articulates the difference between a tutor who is "legitimately helpful and supportive" and one who is a patronizing "Mister Goody-Two-Shoes." He reinforces what tutoring is *not* when he says about his philosophy for writing conferences, "I don't patronize and pat somebody on the head. . . . When you genuinely see a good piece of work done on the page or when you understand from what the student has said that they've gone through a logical process in producing what's on the page, you reinforce that" (1979a).

Correcting Errors

The flip side of "do not cheerlead" is for tutors to avoid being overly critical and nitpicking about writers' work. Finding fault should never be the mission of a one-to-one tutoring session. Sondra Perl's research on composing processes (1978) and Mike Rose's research on writer's block (1984) underscore that obsessing over rules can be damaging to a writer. Premature concern about grammatical correctness and other rules of standard written English may truncate the rhythm of writing or even raise anxiety about writing to a crippling level.

Thus, if a tutor zeroes in only on surface errors—what we refer to as *lower order concerns* (LOCs)—the effect on the writer may be harmful and adverse to the goals of tutoring. Acting as Mr. or Ms. Fix-it by hunting for punctuation errors should be low on a tutor's list of priorities. If a tutoring session is consumed by pointing out a paper's cosmetic flaws, the writer will likely feel demoralized and unwilling to improve the writing. The tutor's job is to encourage the writer to revisit a piece, not to cancel her invitation to write.

Therapy

Tutors may form close bonds with writers, especially if the relationship stretches over a significant time span, but the subject of the interaction should be the writing, not the writer. Do not fall into the trap of becoming the writer's counselor or therapist.

This particular "don't" is tricky, since writers often use writing as an emotional outlet and address highly personal issues and feelings in their work and in their conversations about it. The tutor must recognize the thin line between being an empathetic respondent, which is a useful posture, and being an armchair psychologist, which isn't. In attempting to sort out this distinction, Christina Murphy (1989) makes too strong a case in favor of writing tutors behaving as psychotherapists. She sees a clear connection between the transformative interactions and outcomes that are involved in tutoring and those that are involved in counseling, and even suggests that the terms *tutor* and *student* might be substituted for *therapist* and *client*.

There are parallels between what goes on in a face-to-face writing meeting and in a counseling session. Roger Garrison (1979b), a renowned expert on writing tutorials, explains how the writings of psychologist Carl Rogers shaped his tutoring philosophy:

> I read that book [*Client-Centered Therapy,* 1951] when it was first published; and it had a profound effect on my teaching. Indeed, it's not too much to say that the book, plus other more recent writings of Rogers, was an important intellectual component in my own evolving of the one-to-one approach.

It can be instructive for a writing tutor to borrow some of counseling's nondirective intervention strategies, but it is inappropriate and at times dangerous for the tutor to adopt the role of therapist or healer in a one-to-one conference. Atwell (1998) describes the "delicate touch" necessary when responding to students, a touch whose first principle is "not to become too personal." She underscores that her purpose as a respondent "isn't for me to invite kids' personal problems or offer counsel about them." Murray (1979b) agrees that one of the potential hazards of tutoring is that tutors "get so involved in the subject matter that they may become a therapist." Murray stresses that tutors need to be trained "to make sure they create enough detachment so that they don't become overly involved with the students' subject matter."

If a tutor senses that a student is in troubled waters, she should refer the student to appropriate assistance networks, such as suicide alert and other crisis centers. Unless a tutor has the professional credentials of a therapist, she shouldn't pretend to be one in a writing conference.

Usurping Ownership

The writing tutor must respect the writer's ideas and words. As tempting as it might be for the tutor to rewrite the student's work wholesale by inserting her own information, style, and language (because such ingredients would improve the piece of writing), she should resist doing so, always remembering that she is not the writer's coauthor.

One of Nancy Sommers' (1982) guidelines for responding to writers asserts that the tutor should not appropriate the student's text. Writers should feel welcome to explore their own ideas and find their own ways to express them, without unwelcome intrusions from the tutor. Atwell (1998), too, emphasizes the importance of students maintaining ownership of their work. Murray (1982a) warns that tutors who "pounce on first-draft writing and make corrections . . . take the writing away from the writer." He portrays such heavy-handed tutors as first-draft "kidnappers" who stifle the writer's voice, wrest the responsibility for making meaning out of the writer's hands, and ultimately guide the writer to produce work that is "trivialized, unchallenging, unauthoritative, impersonal, unimportant."

Being an Expert

Diane Stelzer Morrow (1991) changed careers from medicine to teaching. In her discussion of the similarities between being a doctor and being a writing tutor, she describes her pleasant discovery that tutors, unlike doctors, do not need to appear infallible. Morrow's finding is particularly relevant for peer writing tutors, who need not feel pressure to have all the answers, much less the "right" answers. Rather, the peer tutor can help by "nudging" the writer, in a facilitative way, toward routes to the truth, the facts, and the best structural scheme. The tutor should give honest feedback and not feel inadequate if she can't answer a writer's question. Sometimes the best reader is a "dumb reader," one who is not an authority in the subject matter. The tutor can fill that role.

Part of being an effective tutor means equipping writers with strategies for discovering their own answers, perhaps by suggesting a potentially useful website, book, or resource person. By reading widely, the tutor will develop a rich network of materials to refer writers to.

The real expert about the writing is the writer, who knows the subject matter better than the tutor does.

Responding Too Late

When we conduct writing workshops in the world of business and industry, we usually invite participants to bring in samples of writing-in-progress so that we can give them feedback. More often than not, writers instead bring in artifacts from their files—reports from a month back, letters from a year ago—apparently expecting a kind of postgame critique. These writers miss an ideal opportunity to have a private audience with a live reader of a live piece of writing. One of the joys of tutoring is being on hand when the writer needs you. Atwell (1998) calls this constant of writing conferences "the immediacy of response." Murray (1979a) uses the metaphor of writers needing "somebody running along beside them while they have the experience of writing"—the tutor is that runner. Tom Newkirk (1979) has reservations about conferences that are "only a postmortem on a paper."

We are not referring to editing or even proofreading conferences: Those acts are vital to composition, and a final get-together between tutor and writer can result in impressive last-minute fine-tuning. We are referring to conferences that talk about stale writing products, "done deals" that have already been finished. An after-the-fact debriefing about a completed piece of writing is not an effective use of a tutor's skills. The best time for tutors to help is when writers are engaged in the composing process—searching for a subject, starting a draft, revising, and editing. The tutor must be at the writer's side when the writer needs her the most.

The tutor should take advantage, then, of the unique face-to-face intervention that tutoring writers affords, making herself available while the writer is at work rather than waiting until it is too late.

Chapter Four

The Writing and Tutoring Processes

The Writing Process

Whether you are a classroom teacher, a writing center tutor, a workplace trainer, or a parent, you need to have an understanding of the writing process—what writers do and how pieces grow and develop. Much has been learned about the process in the past thirty years that can help tutors understand the complexity of the process and suggest strategies to use with writers during a tutorial. This section reviews both the theory of and research into the writing process, beginning with the insights of researchers from the late 1960s through the early 1980s, who used the methods of psycholinguistics, cognitive psychology, and educational case study, and ending with insights of researchers during the 1980s and 1990s, who used the methods of sociolinguistics, feminism, and cultural studies. As we present this historical unfolding, we also present a second unfolding—from the mind of the writer out to the sociocultural and political context in which writers live and write. Understanding both of these structures—historical and "mind-out-to-culture"—is necessary to understanding the nature of writing and tutoring.

The Writer Writing

Researchers from the late 1960s through the early 1980s (Emig 1969; Perl 1978; Flower and Hayes 1981) focused their attention on the writer writing, an individual performing a complex mental and linguistic act. By observing writers and interviewing them during and after writing, researchers developed a description of the three main stages of the writing process: prewriting, writing, and rewriting. This *stage-process model* was important because it showed that all writers follow the same general path when writing. Before this model was developed, the writing process was thought to be individualistic, with each writer working in a unique way.

This stage-process model was enriched by the development of a *recursive* stage-process model that incorporates the idea that certain stages and the subactivities within them recur during the writing process. For example, a writer might write a paragraph, then rewrite a portion of it, then move on to the next paragraph; *rewriting* is thus both a major stage of the process and a recurring activity during another of the major stages, *writing*. Emphasizing the recursive nature of the writing process allows it to be described in a much more complex way, with stages and embedded subactivities and the writing process becoming multiple writing processes, all similar and yet all different.

In this recursive model, the writing process is still described as having three major stages—prewriting, writing, and rewriting—but each stage is described as having recurring subactivities. *Prewriting* is characterized by planning activities, such as reading related materials from paper or electronic sources; talking to the teacher, tutor, colleagues, or parents; and sketching notes or outlines. Planning activities can occur over and over, even interrupting the writing stage when the writer believes that more reading, talking, and sketching are necessary.

Writing begins at an identifiable moment and usually does not recur unless the writer decides to scrap everything he's written thus far and start over, which happens when completely reformulating a piece seems necessary. Writing itself is not a steady, straight-ahead activity. It is punctuated by hesitations when the writer does projective structuring (anticipating what will be said later) or retrospective review (rereading and rethinking what has already been written). The writer rides the wave of projecting forward while reviewing backward, the balance between the two allowing the current moment of writing.

A writer will hesitate for even more reasons: to consider the spelling of a word; to make a sentence-level style decision about something like how parallel structure in a series of sentences might work out; to consider the piece's macrostructure—how the paragraphs and sections within it are ordered. Any of these hesitations can lead to revising what has been written or what will be written, or to scrapping the piece and making a new beginning.

The recursive stage-process model looks at a writer writing, an observable person producing an observable piece of writing. Other researchers, granting the insightfulness of this observational research, went on to ask about what *can't* be observed—the activities in the writer's mind that are the source of the observable stages and activities. They wanted to know what went on in the writer's head, and they found those cognitive activities to be just as complex as the observable writing activities. The writer's mind is dominated by three cognitive processes—*generating, translating,* and *reviewing*—that are separate but entwined, so that at any moment one might be at the top of the mind and the others moving and rising. Each of the three processes has three major components—*memory, the piece so far,* and *the rhetorical situation* (the interaction of audience and purpose)—that, again, are separate but entwined so all three move into and out of dominance.

These three cognitive processes and three components of writing go together in very complex patterns. For example, a writer might need to generate the appropriate language for a piece—from individual words to the overall language structure—from memory. Of course, the writer would also use memory to supply the issues and ideas that are the content of the piece by searching through past experience, reading, and talking.

The language, language structures, issues, and ideas are then translated into appropriate writing for the given piece, the appropriateness being determined by using memory to generate, translate, and review the meaning of the piece so far and compare it to rhetorical situations involving similar audiences and purposes. All of this mental activity happens within the recursive stage-process model, with the writer prewriting, planning, writing, hesitating, revising—and even scrapping and rewriting—in an instant, over and over, the writer's mind cooking ideas, language, past experiences, and rhetorical specifications.

The Sociocultural and Political Context

From the early 1980s through current studies, researchers have shifted the focus of their work to the wider context in which writers write (Bakhtin 1981; Bruffee 1986; Freire and Macedo 1987). They argue that writers don't use mental and linguistic activities as lone individuals and that writing is never just the result of cognitive and psychological processes: Writers and writing exist within a culture and use a language created by that culture; that is, writers and writing both produce and are a product of wider social and political realities.

When writers write they use a system of symbols created by the culture. In a circular process, the symbol system itself is used to create the culture as writers create and share meanings in writing. Even when writers sit alone at the word processor, they are constantly connected to the society in which they live and write, not just by the socioculturally constructed language they use, but also by the memory that supplies them with culturally derived issues, ideas, language structures, and rhetorical strategies. Writers present their ideas and perspectives in finished pieces they think of as "theirs," when in reality writing is always "theirs/ours": the writer's and the culture's.

Writers and writing are also part of the wider political reality of their world. The idea that written language is part of the political structure may surprise some people, but when writers write they make all kinds of political decisions. Take this book: It is a political act as much as it is a written act or an educational act. We take a political stance just by talking about tutoring, a form of teaching and learning that runs counter to the dominant lecture-and-test form. We are promoting a practice—teaching writing by tutoring writers one-to-one—that reduces the power hierarchy of teacher over student, that sees teaching as best done in collaboration with the learner. These are radical ideas that call power structures into question, a political act for sure. And tutoring is effective, thereby promoting writing ability and the benefits it can bring (school diplomas and college degrees, office promotions, higher grades) for a larger group than the traditional lecture-and-test setting might. This can be threatening to those in power.

Writing is political in more aspects than just the topic the writer chooses. The stance a writer takes with the audience is political, too. We could have written this book as distant experts, university professors, but we've tried to write it from the more democratic stance that we know a good deal about tutoring writing and want to share it with people who, like us, want to help improve others' writing. We aimed for a stance and language that are accessible, helpful, even motivating. We want this book to help writing improve in classrooms, offices, and homes, not to be just another professional publication.

The writing process, then, looks like this: Recursive stage-process activities—prewriting, planning, writing, hesitating, revising, scrapping, and rewriting—occur as the writer's mental and linguistic processes and components cook—generating, translating, and reviewing the text so far and the rhetorical situation (all derived from memory)—all in the context of the sociocultural and political context of *this* writer with *this* piece of writing. The final piece is that this process varies among writers—and within individual writers on different days as they work with different topics, types of writing, audiences, and purposes. And then the tutor enters, smiling because he knows just how complex what he is about to undertake really is.

The Tutoring Process

The Priority of Concerns

There is an overriding priority of concerns in most tutoring sessions. Since all tutoring sessions are geared toward improving a piece of writing within a reasonable time limit and the constraints of the writer's energy level, more serious problems should be addressed first. We set up a two-tier hierarchy of higher order concerns (HOCs) and lower order concerns (LOCs). As the names imply, HOCs are responsible for the more serious problems in a piece of writing, while LOCs are responsible for less serious but still important problems.

HOCs are the features of a piece of writing that exist beyond the sentence level; they include clarity of thesis or focus, adequate development and information, effective structure or organization, and appropriate voice or tone—all important aspects of a piece of writing. LOCs are the features within a sentence, at the level of individual words and punctuation; they include sentence structure and variety, punctuation, grammar and usage, and spelling, elements often made overly important by a society obsessed with correctness.

Three Tutoring Options

Although the basic structure of most tutorial sessions is similar, every encounter with a writer demands an individualized response by the tutor. This book provides reasonable procedures for tutoring sessions, but we encourage tutors to remain flexible with writers and to acquire a tutoring style with which they are comfortable. By observing and interviewing master tutors at work, Tom Reigstad (1980) has identified three tutoring options: *student-centered, collaborative,* and *teacher-centered.* Tutors who are familiar with these options can borrow from any one at any moment during a tutoring session. We recommend the student-centered and collaborative options as being most productive with most writers, but the teacher-centered option has its place in certain circumstances and with certain writers.

Student-centered tutoring. A student-centered tutoring style is desirable because it encourages the writer to do most of the talking and most of the work. The writer even determines the direction of the session and initiates movement to each new phase. The tutor listens a great deal, especially early in the session, asks a few questions, and contributes personal recollections and associations to add to the writer's discovery and development of the subject. Student-centered tutorials are conducted informally, with the writer treated as the tutor's conversational equal. The tutor relies on open-ended and probe-and-prompt questions to draw the writer out to discuss the piece and the process that led to it. The writer then initiates discussion about the issues she sees as problems in the piece, and the tutor suggests strategies for improving the work.

Collaborative tutoring.   Collaborative tutoring allows the tutor to maintain a flexible posture. The tutor encourages the writer, often with open-ended and probe-and-prompt questions, to engage in off-the-paper, exploratory talk and to expand upon undeveloped themes in the paper. As a consequence, the relationship between tutor and writer changes from teacher-student to converser-converser several times during the tutorial. The tutor also moves from talk focused on the paper to off-the-paper talk, then brings the conversation back to the draft by encouraging the student to include ideas from the conversation in the piece. The tutor and writer share equally in the conversation, the problem solving, and the decision making. In collaborative tutoring, however, it is the tutor who initiates the move to a new phase and who usually identifies problem areas on which to focus. A great deal of conference time is spent talking about the writer's composing processes or about information in the draft or the ideas that grow out of it.

Teacher-centered tutoring.   Sometimes time constraints, the nature of the writer, or the nature of the piece dictate that the tutor become more like a traditional teacher, adopting a teacher-centered tutoring style that is direct and that sets the tutor up as an authority and expert. Even though the ultimate goal of a tutoring session is to help the writer, not the piece of writing, there are occasions where a teacher-centered approach is appropriate and valuable. In this type of tutorial, the student sits more passively as the tutor reads through the piece and, often pen in hand, asks questions about mechanical errors, supplying alternatives and the reasons for them when the writer isn't forthcoming about them. The tutor dominates the talk, relying on closed, leading, or yes/no questions, and little of the talk is off-the-paper. The teacher-centered tutor issues directives for revising both HOCs and LOCs.

Tutoring as Chaos, Complexity, and Fuzziness

Tutoring often is complex, seems chaotic, and ends in fuzziness. Some who look at tutoring might criticize it for being so; they might call for more deliberateness, directness, and definition. But there is no need to move in that direction. In fact, if recent scientific theories are right (Hall 1991; Waldrop 1992; Kosko 1993), there might be a real advantage to keep tutoring full of chaos, complexity, and fuzziness. Scientists have developed chaos theory, complexity theory, and fuzzy logic to explain issues in the natural world that were previously difficult to understand, and these theories give us useful metaphors for understanding what happens in tutoring sessions.

The chaos of tutoring writing. Chaos theory asks us to replace the central metaphor of our world and its workings; the world is no longer the Newtonian clock with its cogwheels and levers, rational and predictable: the machine, the computer, the robot. Chaos theory suggests metaphors that are more indeterminate, unpredictable, and random, such as turbulent rivers, weather, and smoke, and demonstrates that exact prediction is impossible in complex systems. One of us once had a predraft conference with a seventh-grade writer who wanted something to write about. When questioned about what he liked, he replied, "WWF wrestling." The tutor said, "Why not write about that?" And the writer did, for the next nine months of the school year, producing the *Wednesday Wrestling Weekly* every week. A conference of less than a minute led to nine months of writing.

We ask tutors to be aware that chaos never repeats itself. When tutors deal with the same writing problems in different pieces—even if it is the same problem in a piece written by the same writer on the same day—exact repetition almost never occurs in a tutoring session.

We train our tutors to have interpersonal skills and a toolbox of strategies that will give them the versatility to move across no-repeat sessions. One of us remembers a tutor saying, "If it's Benny, it's organization. But we never seem to go at it the way we did last time." Chaos theory tells us not to even expect repetition in a system that's as complex as tutoring writing is. Tutoring is not a matter of applying preformed thoughts and actions to the present situation as much as it is of developing a repertoire of interpersonal and pedagogical skills that put the tutor in a general state of readiness.

The complexity of tutoring writing. Complex systems are said to be incompressible—so much so that the thing itself is its own shortest description. Try to describe one day in New York City. We bet that you'll soon throw up your hands and say, "Ahh, just go there for a day and see!" So it is with tutoring. Ask an experienced tutor how he tutors and you'll open the floodgates to hours of stories and strategies and theories. The best way to describe tutoring is to *do* tutoring, and then to talk and try some more. To be able to fully describe tutoring would freeze it and reduce the dynamic diversity that's essential to keeping the system at the edge of chaos, the place of highest potential for learning.

Finally, complex systems can constantly adapt to the environment and its changes. Actions and structures emerge as a result of these adaptations as the interactions of a system's components give rise to new characteristics on the macro or global level. So it is in tutoring: A tutoring session shows emergent adaptation as the session is negotiated and defined through the conversation of tutor and writer. The interactions of writer, piece, and tutor create the overall characteristic of the session, be it dull, valuable, confused, or energetic. As the complex tutoring system operates, adaptations further its progress, create its value, and color its reality for tutor and writer.

The fuzziness of tutoring writing. Fuzzy logic also gives insights into the nature of tutoring by stressing that the world is not right or wrong, one or zero, black or white, but rather shades of gray—not exact, but fuzzy. Fuzzy logic was developed for areas where scientific exactness interfaces with human judgment and emotions. In the fuzzy world, the fuzzy principle rules: Everything is a matter of degree. Bivalent, either/or thinking often makes sense in math and science, but human activity is full of multivalent understandings. Fuzzy logic gives us a perspective from which to see how important shades of gray are in the world of human interactions.

In tutoring there is no right or wrong answer; rather, there is a helpful and reasonable dialogue about the writer's piece. The tutor doesn't lay down rules; he draws out the writer to clarify steps that might improve the student's writing process or written product. Tutoring writers is a fuzzy job about a fuzzy process. The writer needs to learn that the actions she takes in drafting or revising may be the best actions to a degree—a fuzzy degree. The tutor needs to learn that his actions during tutoring are also fuzzy, guiding the writer to a degree, empowering her to participate in setting the session's agenda and to sometimes take the lead. Tutoring sessions are shades of gray in actions and outcomes, and that is good, that is human.

Body Language and the Tutoring Environment

Polished tutors are aware of the messages given by their posture, gestures, and tone of voice, and they learn to manipulate those three areas to ensure the messages are positive. Posture, because it is often seen and assessed from a distance, is the first message the tutor sends to the writer. The tutor should adopt a posture that is alert but relaxed. If the tutor is overly attentive, the writer may perceive it as nervousness, insecurity, or even anger; if the tutor is too relaxed, the writer may take it as indifference or fatigue. In classrooms, writing centers, and offices, tutors should look approachable and never suggest with posture that their own work is more pressing than the tutoring session. The rule for posture is: Look available. Once the tutoring session is underway, the tutor can lean in a bit to show interest and connection.

The tutor's gestures are constantly assessed by the writer. At the first moment of interaction, the tutor should establish eye contact and smile (but remember that eye contact is much less frequent in some cultures than it is in America). Once tutoring is underway, the tutor can nod and use back-channel vocalizations like "yeah" and "uh-huh" to reinforce the nod, showing attention and interest. The tutor should scrupulously avoid gestures and actions that the writer might read as inattention, boredom, or displeasure, such as folded arms, looking past the writer at other people or events, taking a phone call, looking at a clock or watch, yawning, fidgeting, doodling, drumming fingers, and tapping a pen.

The writer reads the tutor's tone of voice, so the tutor should strive for a tone that is both friendly and professional, approachable and efficient. If the tutor sounds harsh, the writer may be intimidated or put off. If the tutor is too warm, the writer may assume that nothing directly useful will happen.

Tutors can use posture, gesture, and tone of voice to send messages that sharpen their tutorial effectiveness. But these messages can be undermined if the environment itself sends different messages. For obvious reasons, the tutoring space should be ample, comfortable, well lighted, and even cheery. In writing centers and offices, the importance of tutoring writing can be communicated powerfully and immediately by the institutional and organizational energy that has gone into the tutoring environment. The environment also communicates by how well it is stocked with writing tools such as computers, printers, software, pens, paper, and reference books.

We would expect a writing center to score high in these areas since tutoring writing is its central mission. Many elementary classrooms set up a tutoring space that's like a learning center or writing place—a separate, private, well-stocked work area with several small tables or desks arranged in pairs. In secondary or college classrooms, the back row of desks can be reserved for writers and their tutors, with pairs moving to the tutoring row when a writer feels a conference is necessary. In classrooms at any level, the entire class can be involved in a writing workshop, making tutoring an organic part of the whole classroom. In an office, a tutoring center can be established at a table or desk that writer and tutor can move to as necessary, or a tutor can have an L- or U-shaped desk with one "arm" reserved for working with the writers who approach. At home, although the kitchen table is probably the favorite place, a separate table or desk can be set up if space allows. There are two last considerations that apply to all tutoring environments: The tutor should sit next to the writer or both should sit at a corner so that both can see the draft, and, whenever possible, a computer should be nearby so that on-screen tutorials are a possibility.

Chapter Five

Tutoring When the Writer Does Not Have a Draft

Sometimes a writer needs help with the writing from ground zero, because he has only the jumbled beginnings of a draft, has not gotten anything written down yet, or has no idea what to write about. The tutor's primary role at this stage is to provide expert help with pre-drafting or prewriting. This chapter suggest a variety of questions the tutor can ask and a variety of strategies she can suggest as she guides the writer through discovering a subject to write about, elaborating on the newly discovered subject with information and ideas, and shaping the information and ideas into the beginnings of a draft.

When a Writer Needs Help Finding a Topic

Tutor Questions

What's the assignment?

Do you have a subject? [If the writer answers "no," ask these questions—]
> What have you been thinking or reading about lately?
> What are you curious to know more about?

Strategies

Writing territories. When a writer has no idea what to write about, suggest that he take ten minutes to generate a list of "writing territories" (Atwell 1998)—that is, a personalized, diverse, and specific list of subjects he has written about already or would like to try writing about, including concerns, memorable incidents, and strong opinions. As Atwell puts it, the items on a writing territories list add up to a writer's "self-portrait." Making such a list enables the writer to brainstorm and explore his own interests, attitudes, and areas of authority—his "territories." (Tom Reigstad's writing territories list is depicted in Figure 5–1.) Then go over the list until you both latch onto an item that is a likely candidate to write further about. Writing territories are similar to Murray's (1984) notion of an "authority list," in which writers brainstorm about things that they are experts in. A nice thing about authority lists and writing territories is that they can be saved and updated periodically, then used as a resource whenever a writer

Figure 5–1
Tom Reigstad's Writing Territories (June 1999)

- the tying a bow dysfunction (a kindergarten problem for male Reigstads . . . or Thank God for Velcro)
- Big 4 basketball—it declined before it barely started
- being an overprotective parent
- the village of Kenmore as "Mayberry, USA"
- memorable snowfalls (including January '99)
- a native Buffalonian living in D.C. . . . Missouri . . . Iowa
- belonging to a book club
- my ex-career as a writing seminar presenter
- impressive business organizations: Saturn; Manhattan Bagel; Target; Stereo Advantage
- the anti-public education pendulum swing: charter schools; budget cuts; taxpayer groups
- what it must be like having parents who are teachers
- why anyone besides gym teachers would become school administrators
- comparing Quality Market and Tops: a sociologist's dream, down to the cat food
- whatever happened to McDonald's efficiency
- playing pick-up ball as a kid
- adult rituals of softball and basketball
- the struggle and obsession to be physically fit
- what the Army was able to teach a 22-year-old with a master's degree and an attitude
- getting your first teaching job at the high school you graduated from

shows up for a tutoring session not knowing what to write about.

Free writing. An excellent technique for helping the writer get something down on paper is to ask her to write for ten minutes about anything that pops into her head. She must write without stopping, without going back to correct anything. If she can't think of anything, she should keep writing the words "I can't think of anything to write" until something else jumps in. This exercise, popularized by Peter Elbow (1981), liberates the writer from her internal critic and allows pure discovery of thought on paper (or computer terminal screen). After ten minutes, look at the results together and pick out intriguing ideas or attractive, surprising phrases that might form the basis of a thesis for a full paper.

Figure 5-1, continued

- the romance and reality of being a writer/editor at the Courier-Express
- the accidental teacher
- the physical and psychological traces of a Norwegian bloodline
- confessions of a snack food king
- our life with Portia the Christmas cat
- how two boys—Luke and Leif—can be so alike, yet so different
- my Dad as hero—one special day of unloading incredibly heavy office furniture at UB and then pitching an entire baseball game; taking on the Big C
- on avoiding writing
- on avoiding high school reunions
- the feeling of a Buffalo native who feels rootless
- the pull of a Protestant upbringing (the inexplicable desire to sing all 8 verses of the old-time hymns) while of necessity attending Catholic church
- my preference for reading nonfiction and aversion to drama
- getting caught innocently in the beanie baby craze
- the greed of garage sales
- is it possible to get through Flag Day ceremonies or Memorial Day parades without choking up?
- the constant noise assault of power tools in Kenmore—some places around the country have zones preventing leaf blowers
- cell phone abuse (Blockbuster story; cars) and backlash (phone rage—Japan has no cell phone areas)
- why do TV Guides have to be collectible?

Rapid sketches. Another useful brainstorming technique is the rapid sketch. As described by Donald Graves (1996), the writer begins by taking about four minutes to make a list of what has transpired in his life over the last two or three days, then looks over the list and chooses one item to write more about for another five minutes. Graves emphasizes that the writer should adhere to these guidelines: Write rapidly, change nothing, lower your standards. Rereading one rapid sketch (or a series of them) helps the writer become sensitive to issues in his own life that are worth exploring.

Conversation. Don't overlook the power of simply engaging in natural conversation with the writer, bantering back and forth about mutual interests such as music, sports, or current political events. The writer may make a connection with a problem you have or an author you admire or a brand of sneaker you prefer—and seize on it as something interesting to write about. As you talk over possible topics with the writer, try Atwell's (1998) suggestion of scribbling snippets of the conversation on sticky notes so that the writer has a rough record of this productive oral brainstorming to use later.

Free talking. Free talking isn't quite the oral counterpart of free writing, but a sequence of steps devised by Robert Zoellner (1969) to combine oral and written brainstorming so that a writer gradually narrows down a manageable topic. Ask the writer to brainstorm ideas aloud for ten minutes, recording her talk on an audiotape, then to play back the tape and transcribe relevant portions. Have the writer then talk about and elaborate on the transcription, continuing to record, then play that second taping and extract salient points and write them down. This talk-write-retalk-rewrite sequence should move the writer from sheer brainstorming toward focused consideration of a subject.

Doodling or sketching. Author Gabriel Garcia Marquez (1984) once commented that his interest in writing was cultivated by drawing cartoons: "Before I could read or write I used to draw cartoons at school and at home . . . in the genesis of all my books there's always an image." Marquez even compiled a collection of photographs that he referred to for beginning points in his writing projects. Visual thinking can help verbal thinking. Ask the writer to draw or sketch something as he lets his mind wander. He may notice a theme or pattern developing in the doodle, which can prove to be a starting point for writing that is a personal reflection or attitude. Graves (1994) reminds us of the special place that drawing has for children as a warm-up to writing. He has observed that children use their drawings as a rehearsal for the written text that follows.

Figure 5-2
3 x 5 Card Exercise

Working for a Moving Company		
skins	come-along	carry
pads	Johnny bar	roll-a-life machines
overseas crates	reefer dolly	weight
packing	palletizing	scale
picking	containerize	(Anjon's)
base	crate	out-of-towner
dolly	mats	estimate
two-wheeler	cartons	long haul
four-wheeler	tape guns	piano board

Anjon's	
Two Trip Breakfast	attractive to drivers
Country Breakfast specials ($1.55)	Joe K.'s 4 sandwiches
slow service (surprisingly)	Walden Ave.
not crowded	coffee
friendly waitress	juice
cheap	toast
lunch specials	2 eggs
huge parking lot	home fries

Anjon's restaurant on Walden near Transit is a popular breakfast and lunch eatery for truckers. Although this truck stop might lack good food and fast service, it makes up for it in friendly waitresses, a cheap menu, and that most valuable commodity for tractor trailer drivers—ample parking space. My two dining experiences there have been mixed. The two breakfast specials I've ordered—including coffee, juice (in a thimble-like glass), two eggs, toast, and home fries—for $1.55, have been average. But the waitresses have made it pleasant by joking with me and my fellow workers/diners. In fact, when one crewman ordered four grilled cheese sandwiches for lunch one day, the cook even came out to kid him about his appetite

Composing Exercise

Complete each of the following steps on a separate three-by-five card. A sample response to each step is given on the facing page.

Step 1. Think of an experience, a person, or a place and list 20–25 specific details (words, phrases, impressions) about it on Card 1.

Step 2. Circle the most interesting or surprising detail on Card 1. On Card 2, provide more information about what you have circled. Drive yourself to make this new list of short specific details as long as possible.

Step 3. Use the list of details on Card 2 to write whole sentences, actually a rough draft, on Card 3. Put the information you assembled on Card 2 into a meaningful order on Card 3. Look for patterns among the specific details, ways to link them together, and ways to organize them. Turn the details into sentences.

Step 4. Edit and proofread Card 3. Correct grammar, usage, spelling, and punctuation. If necessary, recopy what you have written.

Three-by-five card exercise.   This activity helps the writer not only to brainstorm possible subjects, but to narrow her thinking down to one subject and get started writing on it. Figure 5–2 illustrates this exercise.

Heightening the writer's alertness.   Sometimes a tutor can help a writer find a topic by keeping her writer's antennae attuned to possibilities in the world around her. Writers need a reminder, a jog, to tell them how rich and varied their own lives are. They need to become more aware of the unique hidden in the mundane, especially where least expected. You might share this anecdote of how E. L. Doctorow (1988) came to write *Ragtime*: He was facing the wall of his study in New Rochelle, New York, as he sat groping for ideas. Desperate, he started to write about the wall, which led to writing about the house, which had been built in 1906. Those jottings progressed to a description of the era and became the beginning of a novel. You might also pass on the advice of Verlyn Klinkenborg (1992), who implores writers to "brood," to be in a constant state of writing readiness by being open to the surprise appearance of an internal writing episode popping into their daily routines: "The capacity for editing sentences in your head while waiting in a supermarket line is eminently useful." Tom Brown (1983) teaches writers who are out in the field to use "spattervision" to increase their observation of features of nature. Rather than focusing on particular objects, the writer lets her eyes glaze over slightly and tries to take in everything within a wide half-circle. Brown also suggests several sighting and journal-writing activities to help writers become more alert to discovering new things in familiar landscapes.

When a Writer Has a Topic, But No Draft

Tutor Questions

What's the assignment?

Do you have a subject? [If the writer answers "yes," ask the following questions—]

What do you know about the subject?

What don't you know about the subject?

How can you look for connections among the tidbits that you already know that might suggest new directions?

Strategies

Cubing. *Cubing* teaches the writer to approach a subject from six perspectives (like the six sides of a cube):

1. *Describe* the subject by jotting down ideas about its color, shape, size, origin, parts, and makeup.
2. *Compare* the subject to something else—what is it like or unlike?
3. *Associate* the subject with other things by making personal connections.
4. *Analyze* the subject by responding to questions like: How is it made? How are its parts related? Where is it going? Where did it come from?
5. *Apply* the subject by writing about what can be done with it, or what uses it has.
6. *Argue* for or against the subject by choosing a side and defending it.

Twenty questions.   Teach the writer to ask the right questions and jot down responses to the questions as she explores their subject. Figure 5–3 shows a handy list of twenty questions that the writer can run through systematically to generate ideas about the subject (substitute the subject for "X" on the list). Note that not every question will be relevant to a given subject.

Particle/wave/field perspectives.   The writer can apply the subject to a series of prompts devised by Richard Young, Alton Becker,

Figure 5–3
Twenty Questions

---

1. How is X different from things in your personal experience?
2. What does X mean?
3. How is X made or done?
4. X used to be _____, but now is _____.
5. Where does X occur or appear?
6. What is the primary function of X?
7. Why does X occur?
8. What does X cause or influence?
9. What are the consequences of X?
10. What are the types of X?
11. How does X compare with Y?
12. How is X different from things in your vicarious experience?
13. How is X different from what you expected?
14. What is the present status of X?
15. What kind of person is X?
16. What is the value of X?
17. When does X occur?
18. What happens just before/after X?
19. What is likely to be true of X in the future?
20. What case can be made for/against X?

and Kenneth Pike (1970). Viewing the subject from three perspectives can help uncover areas to write about that might otherwise have been overlooked. This system prompts the writer to look at the subject in terms of *particles* (as if it were static), *waves* (as if it were dynamic), and *fields* (as if it were a network of relationships). Young, Becker, and Pike's prompts include these:

> Particle: What are the subject's contrastive features? How much can the subject vary before becoming something else? How should it be classified?

> Wave: What physical features distinguish the subject from similar objects or events? How is it changing? How does it interact with and merge into its environment?

> Field: How are the subject's components organized in relation to one another and in time and space? How do particular instances of the system vary? What is the subject's position in the larger system?

Burke's pentad. Kenneth Burke (1945) devised a five-part question-asking activity that is especially useful to writers examining human motivation in terms of actions and their results. If you're working with a writer who needs to compose a profile or a response to a literary character, having the writer take notes on the pentad questions can be very productive:

> Act: What was done?

> Scene: When or where was it done?

> Agent: Who did it?

> Agency: How did he or she do it? What means or instruments were used?

> Purpose: Why did she or he do it?

Looping. Looping allows writers to explore in writing what they know about a subject, to stop and reflect on what they just wrote, and then to write further based on their new understanding (Elbow 1981). Ask the writer to spend from five to ten minutes writing whatever he knows about the subject, then to read the writing over and compose a single sentence that expresses the most important idea in it. That sentence then becomes the focus of another five-to-ten-minute directed free writing, which again is read over, reflected on, and summarized in a sentence. This cycle may take place as many as three times, at which point the writer should have enough understanding of the subject to be able to settle on a focus.

Titles.   Some writers who have a subject in hand find it helpful to formulate several possible titles before starting a draft, which is a way to establish parameters for the paper. In his days as a freelance writer, Murray (1995) would start writing an article by brainstorming from a hundred to a hundred and fifty possible titles: "Each title was a window into the draft I might write." Share Murray's recommendations and those of others (Herrscher 1995; Meyer 1988) who describe title-writing as an indispensable method of narrowing a subject. Recommend the following possibilities to nudge the writer toward experimenting and fishing for titles:

1. Write a title that is a question beginning with "how" or "why."
2. Write a title that is a question beginning with "is" or "are," "do" or "does," or "will."
3. Write a title that begins with an "-ing" verb.
4. Write a title that begins with "on."
5. Write a one-word title.
6. Write a two-word title.
7. Think of a familiar saying, or the title of a book, song, or movie that might fit the subject you are going to write about, then twist it by changing a word or creating a pun on it.
8. Find two titles that you have jotted down that you might use together in a double title (title and subtitle), then join them with a colon.

Clustering.   Ask the writer to write her topic in the middle of a sheet of paper and circle it; then write ideas related to that subject, circle them, and connect them to the main circle; then write ideas related to those ideas, circle them, and join them to the relevant ideas; and so on.

Point-of-view mapping.   Murray (1984) suggests this vehicle to help writers find a focus by moving around the subject and taking quick notes about the place from which the subject is observed. The writer writes the subject in the middle of a sheet of paper; jots down various points of view that might provide different perspectives and sources of information about the subject in a circle around the subject; then draws an arrow from each point of view to the subject in the middle. This gives the writer, with a quick glance, various points from which he may view the subject. (As discussed in the next chapter, you can recommend other kinds of mapping activities once the writer has a draft in progress.)

When a Writer Has a Partial Draft

After successfully steering a writer through the tricky waters of brainstorming with or without a subject, you will probably be called upon to help her incorporate some of the materials she has gathered into the beginnings of a draft.

Leads. One way to put the drafting process in motion is to show writers how to formulate the journalistic *lead*. Garrison (1985) suggests eleven leads tutors should be familiar with: anecdote, startling statement, narrative, summary, quotation, question, description, general statement, analogy, statement of purpose, and news lead. If the writer has difficulty starting to write or has written portions of a discovery draft, run through these leads until one strikes the writer as a useful hook to hang the draft onto.

Repeating a key word. Once the inertia of beginning a draft is overcome, encourage the writer to sustain the flow at all costs. One technique we described in an earlier monograph (Reigstad and McAndrew 1984) teaches the writer to force the draft along by building each sentence around a key word or phrase from the previous sentence. This device may not produce the best writing, but it keeps the draft rolling, which is the crucial objective. Consider the paragraph below. The writer got stuck after the third sentence, but by repeating a key word (underlined) was able to push through temporary writer's block and move on to the next sentence—and the next—until a more natural rhythm was regained.

> *Hjemkomst* means "homecoming" in Norwegian. And that's exactly what the aptly-named American-built replica of a Viking <u>ship</u> did during the summer of 1982. The <u>ship</u> was handmade in Duluth and began its transatlantic trip from <u>Knife River</u>, Minnesota, on Lake Superior in May. From <u>Knife River</u>, the Hjemkomst longship sailed through the <u>Great Lakes</u>, with stops in Detroit, Cleveland and Buffalo. The ship left the <u>Great Lakes</u> at the Erie Barge Canal and proceeded to <u>New York City</u>. From <u>New York</u>, the crew launched the last leg of its trip home to Bergen, Norway. The 76 1/2-foot, square-sail vessel completed the 3,500 mile voyage triumphantly in mid-July, but not until experiencing several harrowing episodes.

Framing. If identifying an opening line and keeping the draft rolling present challenges for writers, finding an appropriate exit can be even more difficult. Be alert to the possibilities of *framing* when a logical closing to a draft is not apparent. Framing links the conclusion and opening of a draft by returning to a word, image, theme, or impression that was mentioned in the lead. This device both helps the writer and leaves the reader with a pleasing sense of closure. In the conclusion of his essay about novelist Ken Kesey, Henry Allen's (1975) echoing of the opening is descriptive of the setting and weather, but most particularly of Kesey's hat:

> *Opening:* Ah, yes, feeding the cows. Ken Kesey, at 38, all genial and hulking in his dungaree jacket, his big, tough Buddha face goofy under an ear-flapped green-and-yellow knit cap, strides out through the pasture mud to feed his 26 beef cows, a bale of hay sagging from each hand.

> *Closing:* Kesey tugs on his onion-spire, ear-flapped, Tibetan-style green-and-yellow knit cap, and they rush out into the rain.

Tutoring Strategies for Preventing Writer's Block

- Be sure that the writer doesn't edit prematurely. Blocked writers often interrupt the flow of their writing by fussing too early with elements like comma placement or spelling.

- Help the writer "break out" and take risks (see the discussion of "Grammar B" in Chapter 8). Writers who follow rigid and inappropriate rules for writing are sometimes plagued by self-consciousness and inertia.

- Suggest that a writer make a writing appointment with herself (literally, in her weekly planning calendar) and keep it.

- On in-depth writing projects, urge the writer to write as many parts of the project as possible early on (boilerplate stuff, for example). When you help writers to write early, creating the final version is a matter of fitting completed parts together, which is a much less intimidating job than assembling an entire first draft from start to finish.

- Suggest that a reluctant writer use a warm-up ritual. Most productive writers rely on habits to get them started. Ernest Hemingway sharpened twenty pencils. Thornton Wilder took a long walk. Michael Crichton eats a particular meal, a different one for each book.

- If a writer is struggling, recommend switching tools. If his fingers are motionless at the computer keyboard, he might open up by using a pad and pencil instead (or vice versa).

Chapter Six

What Tutoring Is
Models and Strategies

This chapter discusses responding to a writer's work in ways that address higher order concerns (HOCs), lower order concerns (LOCs), and the piece as a whole. The HOC and LOC sections model specific tutorials, while the section about addressing the piece as a whole presents feedback techniques and strategies.

Higher Order Concerns

Higher order concerns (HOCs), which are central to the meaning and communication of the piece, are matters of thesis and focus, development, structure and organization, and voice. These areas are important in the tutorial because they are central to the piece of writing. It makes sense for tutors and writers to begin with HOCs because improvements in these areas can dramatically change a piece. Even if writers may want to talk about other issues, tutors can honor the writer's desires and still move in the direction of these most important HOCs.

Thesis/Focus Tutorial

With sixty years of teaching and consulting experience between us, we have found certain problems to be common among English 101 writers. One of the most common is thesis/focus. (Another is development, discussed in the next section). Having a clear thesis and a precise focus is essential to good writing and helps the writer see what is essential to include. Too often, writers, especially in early drafts, write down lots of information without considering how it is related to what they want to say. Other times, writers stick to only what is directly related to what they want to say, but what they want to say is too broad and panoramic in conception.

It is crucial that tutors be ready and able to work with writers on their thesis or focus. Whether the piece is an essay for English 101 or a seventh-grade history report, thesis/focus should be the first thing on the tutor's agenda. Tutors can use many strategies and questions to help writers clarify their thesis and sharpen their focus.

Tutor Questions

- What's the central issue of your piece?

- What's the one dominant impression you want your piece to make?

- When the reader is finished reading, what do you want him to walk away with?

- If your roommate, colleague, or sibling walked up to you and asked what you were writing about, what would you say?

Strategies

- *One-sentence summary.* One strategy that is both easy and useful is Elbow's (1973) "one-sentence summary." Ask the writer to make a one-sentence summary of the piece. Usually one of two things happens: If the writer has difficulty writing the summary, intervene to discuss the reasons for the difficulty. If he writes the summary easily, relying on what is in his head or what he thinks the piece is about, compare the summary directly to the actual paper, showing where each says things that are not in the other. Summarizing requires conceptualization and the concomitant distinguishing of major issues and minor ideas, essential to zeroing in on a clear thesis or precise focus.

- *Nutshelling and teaching.* Linda Flower's (1981) "nutshelling and teaching" activity also requires the writer to make decisions about major issues and minor ideas. Ask the writer to orally explain the essence of the piece while you take notes. Then, working from your notes, orally express that essence back to her. Discuss and negotiate the expression of the essence until the writer agrees that you have captured the essence, then ask her to role-play being a teacher who is trying to teach the essence to an audience that is like the writer's audience for the piece. This process of explaining, negotiating, and teaching requires the writer to sort through the major and minor levels of the piece.

▪ *Talk aloud.* Muriel Harris (1996) describes another oral exercise that can be used to help the writer see problems with a thesis or focus. (Oral exercises are particularly helpful with most writers since most people have far more oral language experience than written language experience.) Read the writer's paper silently, interrupting your reading to talk aloud about what you're seeing in the paper. Have the writer take notes. This process lets the writer see how the paper drifts from focus to focus. When you've finished reading, ask, "Okay, so what is the paper about?" In the process of answering, the writer notes the lack of precise focus. He not only decides what the focus of the paper is (probably by establishing a hierarchy to the points the focus drifts among), but often finds that this paper contains the seed for one or more future papers because some of the points deserve to be major issues in their own paper. Working on thesis/focus can sometimes be a heuristic for discovering future paper topics.

▪ *Make a promise.* Harris also describes a "promise" strategy. Explain that a thesis or focus is like a promise made to the reader. Ask the writer to complete this statement: "I promise that I will talk about _____ in this (or these) ways," listing the major ideas used in the draft and evaluating how well each helps the piece fulfill the promise. As in the "talk aloud" exercise, the writer has the opportunity to create an appropriate hierarchy for the ideas and their relationship to the central issue, and oral language is used to mediate both the revision of the current draft and, ultimately, the student's growth in writing. As with all the strategies described, it is not the procedure itself that powers the tutoring session, but rather the conversational interaction in which the strategy is set. The questions and comments the tutor makes are at the heart of the success of the tutoring session.

▪ *Create a headline or bumper sticker.* Ask the writer to give her piece a headline or to make up a bumper sticker based on the piece. Either of these requires that the writer find the one thing that is central to the piece and say something about it. A title can just be a subject ("Causes of the Civil War"), but a headline or bumper stickers has a subject and says something about it ("Deep Creek Lake Rated Best Vacation Spot"; "_____ Is Not a Family Value"). Identifying the subject helps the writer create the hierarchy necessary to nail down the focus by locating the single most essential issue; saying something about the subject lets her begin to understand what ideas might be included in the piece because they fit what she wants to say.

Example of Thesis/Focus Tutorial. Here's an example of how the thesis/focus strategies might work. A student wrote about a lacquered wooden box that her grandfather had made for her grandmother. The piece opened with a detailed description of the box, talked about how her grandfather had made it, then described how much her grandfather and grandmother were in love. The piece finished with how her grandmother uses the box today.

The tutor drew her out to find which of the four issues she really wanted to foreground. She said that she wanted to show the box to the others in class; so, the opening description was the key part and the rest was added just to "fill it out." Once the tutor helped her clarify that showing the box was important, he moved on to development strategies to help the student develop her description of the box so that she would not feel the need to fill the piece out with unrelated information. If the student had said that she wanted two or more of the four main ideas as her focus, the tutor could work with her on creating first an introduction that would show how the ideas went together, then transitions to hold them together.

Effective tutorials on thesis/focus are a combination of using a strategy and conversing about the results of that strategy. The headline or bumper sticker strategy could be used for that same lacquer box paper. If the student wanted to show the box to the class, her headline might be "Beautiful Lacquer Box Created by Pittsburgh Man," or her bumper sticker might be "Lacquer Boxes Don't Lack Anything." Each of these suggests that the appearance of the box is the central issue, so the tutor could ask why the other three ideas were there. But if the headline was "Pittsburgh Man Makes Beautiful Lacquer Boxes," the part of the piece about how her grandfather made the box might be the central idea. Or if her bumper sticker said "Love Is a Lacquer Box," the student may see her grandparents' love as central.

Whatever the writer's central ideas, these strategies are a way to start discussing the necessity of clarifying the thesis/focus.

Development Tutorial

Development is a crucial feature of any piece of writing. Writers gain insight into what points to develop and how to develop them when they work on thesis/focus, and they gain even further insight when they work on organization/structure (discussed below). But often a piece has development as a primary problem: Its thesis is clear and its structure is reasonable, but it just doesn't say enough. First drafts often suffer from underdevelopment because the writer is laying out what he wants to say, scanning the topography of his ideas and sketching a map. Development problems also arise because many writers rely on their oral language experience as a first guide for writing, not realizing that writing must be much more explicit and specific than speech because it has none of the tone of voice or contextual features of speech.

Whether students are laying out ideas in a cursory fashion or writing like speech, tutors will see many drafts that need to be developed. Tutors can use number of strategies and questions to help writers find and express ideas to fill out underdeveloped papers and to get the writer to start reflecting on development problems.

Tutor Questions

- Tell me more.

- Point to places where you think a reader might want you to tell more.

- If you read this aloud to a few readers, what do you think their first questions would be about?

- If black were the color of the parts with lots of information, gray the color of those with less information, and white those with even less information, what color would this part of the piece be?

Strategies

- *Focused free writing.* We train tutors to use an adaptation of Elbow's (1973) idea of free writing that we call "focused free writing." Ask the writer to focus on a portion of the draft that needs development, writing anything and everything he can remember—words, phrases, full sentences—not worrying about spelling or punctuation, just writing. If a writer has written about a football game and has said nothing about the fans in the stands, he may decide that details about them would add color and excitement to the description of the game. Ask the writer to free write for about five minutes on everything he can remember about the fans in the stands. Decide together where the new information might fit, then have the writer shape it into coherent sentences and insert it into the draft.

- *Oral composing.* Oral composing can help the writer develop a draft or part of a draft. Instruct the writer, "Tell—off the top of your head—what you *think* you *might* write. Speak as if you were talking to yourself." Take notes while the writer speaks. Like focused free writing, this exercise helps the writer shape relevant ideas, phrases, and sentences that can be incorporated into the draft where development is thin. If the paper needs further development after oral composing, do a second round of oral composing.

▪ *Mapping.* Emily Meyer and Louise Smith (1987) suggest using mapping to help writers develop a portion of the piece or the piece as a whole. You can do the mapping as you listen to the writer talk about her topic, or the writer can do it herself as a way of playing with the lay of the land of her ideas and issues. Mapping isn't just list making, it is a graphic and visual technique that forces the writer to decide which of the ideas in the piece are important and how they are related to each other. As the writer or tutor adds a word or phrase to the developing graphic, the relationship of that word or phrase to all other entries must be considered. Lines are used to connect entries with each other, suggesting their relationships. Graphic devices such as thick, dotted, or double lines; circles and rectangles; arrows; and shading or colors can be added to say more about the relationships. Drawing a map can lead the writer to making real discoveries about the topic, including that the issues and ideas she originally thought important aren't any longer and may be deleted. Once all the entries and relationships have been stirred and restirred, you may want to redraw the map to make it more sensible. We discourage redrawing graphically (unless the mapping is being done using software that makes it easy), because clarity can be achieved by doing the redrawing in writing. Throughout the process, keep the door to exploration and discovery open by avoiding preconceived or canned visualizations and premature closure or editing.

▪ *Matrices.* Matrices are common devices in research and data analysis. For tutoring sessions, matrices are most often two-dimensional, with one axis listing important issues or ideas, the other listing what is known about them. One writing center used matrix "skeletons" that a tutor or writer could grab during a tutoring session and use to crate a matrix specific to the piece of writing being discussed. You can create a matrix while the writer talks, or the writer can create one as a way to think about the topic. Matrices are powerful analytic tools since they require that major categories of issues be created and related. They are probably best to use when the writer knows a lot about the topic, so much so that his problem may be displaying all his knowledge at any given moment. Matthew Miles and Michael Huberman (1984), discussing matrices as research data analysis tools, suggest three matrices that are useful in getting a handle on understanding phenomena: *role matrices,* which lay out the roles people play along one axis; *time matrices,* which use a chronology style to show beginning, middle, and end or past, present, and future; and *effects matrices,* which display the major effects of a phenomenon. The three types can be combined (roles over time, effects by roles, etc.). Use matrices with caution: Making a good one requires that the writer know a lot about the topic. If he doesn't, some of the other development strategies may be more useful and productive.

▪ *Playing your thoughts.* Linda Flower and John Hayes (1977) describe a number of strategies for generating ideas that they call "playing your thoughts." They include in this category a traditional favorite among creative thinkers—brainstorming, the oral and non-judgmental sharing of ideas, stimulated by the tutor's and writer's associative play off each other's ideas as they emerge. They also include staging a scenario (role-playing) as a way to develop ideas, especially narratives or descriptions of people's interactions. In role-playing, writer and tutor take on roles and invent dialogue as a way to explore the words, gestures, facial expressions, and positions likely to be used by the people in the writer's piece. Flower and Hayes also describe playing out an analogy ("This topic is like X"), in which tutor and writer extend the topic by working out one or more analogies to things the writer already knows well ("increasing sales is like playing the infield"). Flower and Hayes finish by reminding tutors that sometimes pieces are best developed by resting, getting away from the topic and doing something else.

Example of a Development Tutorial.   A student came to the writing center with a paper about Raystown Lake, a large recreational lake in central Pennsylvania. The paper was short (less than a page), so the tutor was on the alert for development possibilities. The piece opened with a three-line description of the lake, then covered boating, swimming, fishing, hiking, bicycling, and camping. Only one of the topics received more than two sentences: Fishing stretched to five. The tutor noticed the imbalance and asked, "When you go to Raystown, what do you spend most of your time doing?" She received the expected answer: "Fishing, I suppose." The tutor thought that the problem with the piece was not with development but with thesis/focus—the writer wanted to write about fishing at Raystown but felt obligated to mention all the other activities too. But when the tutor said, "If you spend most of your time fishing, why did you include these other things that you don't do often?" the answer was quick and firm: "Because I want to talk about all the things you can do there." The tutor saw that the problem was with development after all—the writer really did want to describe all the activities a visitor could do.

The tutor decided to use oral composing to develop the thinnest elements. She said to the writer, "I've never been there. Why don't you tell me about boating, swimming, and all those things. I'll take notes in case we can use any of this stuff in the paper." After an almost twelve-minute monologue by the writer, the tutor had almost one and a half pages of notes about all the activities. The student noticed this and said, "Whoa, your notes are longer than my paper. I guess I better make it longer." The tutor said, "Good idea. You can use all the stuff in these notes."

What if the tutor had used a different strategy? She probably chose the best one in oral composing. She could have had the student do focused free writing to develop each idea in turn, but doing focused free writing seven times in a row would have been burdensome. Mapping seems like a possibility, but it is best applied to situations where the tutor wants the writer to discover the relationships between major ideas and develop material about each. In this piece all the ideas are parallel—they are all activities at Raystown. A matrix would be necessary because careful analysis is not the issue, and a matrix with just one dimension turns out to be more like a list than a matrix. Brainstorming would have generated material but no written record for the writer to use during revision. Role-playing is best for pieces that are focused on human interaction. Completing the analogy might have yielded some insight but would be burdensome to do seven times. Resting is probably what the writer had done too much of already. This successful tutoring session was the result of the tutor's choosing the most appropriate strategy.

Structure/Organization Tutorial

Tutors will frequently work with a writer whose draft has a clear thesis/focus, is well developed, and has appropriate voice/tone, but that could be improved, sometimes dramatically, by restructuring or reorganizing. All the bricks are there; now they need to be made into a fireplace. Structure and organization problems often exist because the writer simply has not thought about the topic enough to see the connections. Sometimes the ideas aren't connected explicitly enough to the thesis/focus; or the logic of the connections between major subparts is fuzzy; or the internal structure/organization of the subparts or paragraphs lacks explicitness or logic. Structure and organization problems can be dealt with using any of the strategies below.

The overall goal of the tutoring for structure/organization is to have the writer become aware of the problems, so we recommend the tutor use strategies that will reveal the structure/organization separately from the actual language, which the writer has often not been able to see past. Once the structure/organization is more visible, the tutor can begin to question the writer about revising it, noting changes in order or hierarchy, repetitions, and deletions or additions. As Irene Clark (1985) reminds us, the final question for the tutor is always "why?"—why did the writer choose this structure/organization. Structure and organization don't just happen as we write, certainly not in later drafts; they are a conscious and adaptable feature of written pieces that the writer can manipulate for her purposes.

Tutor Questions

- Tell me how you tied each part/subpart to the thesis/focus.

- What do you think a reader would see as the major parts of your piece?

- Do you think the piece could be significantly improved by reordering the major parts or the subparts of a specific section?

- Do you think the piece could be improved by making sure that the divisions between the parts are more noticeable to the reader?

Strategies

- *Just talk about it.* Often drafts that seem poorly organized are really just preliminary; the writer hasn't reflected carefully about the thesis/focus. Holding a simple conversation that asks for a statement of the thesis and the major issues within it may be enough to have the writer see the inadequacy of an early draft. Frequently, writers also refine their thesis/focus and develop their draft with issues that were missed in the work that lead to the present draft. What appear as structure/organization problems often disappear the first time the writer thinks through a piece fully.

- *Skeleton.* This strategy is a cousin to outlining, but we call it "making a skeleton" because so many students have bad associations with outlining, which was over-stressed in English classes for years. The numbering of levels that is part of traditional outlining is discarded so that the result is a vertical, two-level list that makes the parts of the piece visible in a way that can be the basis of discussion. To make a skeleton, draw up, or have the writer draw up, a vertical list of the major ideas, including under each its minor supporting ideas. One of the advantages of the skeleton is that it can be sketched quickly and casually, so it need not overpower the rest of the tutorial.

- *Tree diagram.* Beverly Clark (1985) and others recommend creating a tree diagram to reveal the structure/organization of a piece. A tree is a kind of visual outline that combines the levels of a skeleton with the tangibility of mapping, producing a vertical diagram. Ask the writer to write the thesis/focus at the top center of a sheet of paper held sideways. One level below, the writer records the major issues or ideas of the piece, connecting each to the statement of thesis/focus with a line. The writer adds a third level of minor and supporting ideas below the row of major ideas, drawing a line to connect each minor idea to the major idea it supports. Finally, the writer clusters the explanatory ideas for each of the minor supporting ideas on a fourth level and connects them to their related idea. The graphic and visual nature of the tree diagram makes it more acceptable to students who are burned out on outlining.

▪ *Coloring.* Irene Clark (1985) recommends coloring sentences that are related to the same major ideas and should, therefore, ultimately be grouped together. Using a supply of colored pens or highlighters, ask the writer to underline or highlight each sentence that contains ideas related to the different minor ideas. Then ask for a revision that groups the colors into sections. Use further conversation to deal with what the order or hierarchy among the different sections should be.

▪ *Outlining.* Traditional outlining has at least two advantages for tutors. First, almost everyone knows how to do it, so no time need be spent on teaching the strategy itself. Second, the numbering and lettering typical of outlining allow for a kind of shorthand to be used when discussing a piece: "Are 2c and 3b really the same thing?" "What about an order like 2, 4, 1, 3?" "Should 2 be under 1, not its equal?"

▪ *Transitions.* Upon closer examination, you may find that a piece that seems disorganized is really suffering from implied or idiosyncratic transitions between major ideas and the thesis/focus; between the minor ideas and their related major idea; or both. First ask the writer to use one of the strategies for making the structure/organization more visible. Then ask how and why the various major parts are connected, in each case calling for an explicit word or phrase to act as a transition. We supply our tutors with a short list of transitions (available in most writing handbooks) that the writer can choose from at each idea boundary.

Example of a Structure/Organization Tutorial. In a tutorial between a trained peer tutor (a college senior) and a freshman that took place at a university writing center, the writer brought in a draft of a summary of a magazine article about a small religious book publishing company. The writer expected to get quick proofreading advice from the tutor. But after the tutor listened to the author read the summary aloud, he immediately recognized that the draft lacked coherence. The facts from the original magazine article were there, apparently reproduced simply and dryly in the order in which they had appeared, so that the writer's summary had no sense of prioritizing or identifying the central point of the article, which was that the press had survived thirty years of adversity, including stiff competition and labor strife. So the tutor went to work, trying to help the writer reshape the summary into a format that emphasized the controlling point of the article and highlighted some of the other significant points.

The tutor started by asking the writer to reconsider the opening paragraph and to include in it some sense of the organization's history, the long fight between labor and management. The tutor asked, "How could you rearrange it chronologically?" The problem was, though, that the writer still felt married to the existing draft and at first seemed willing only to reshuffle its paragraphs. The tutor patiently suggested that the writer block off and number each paragraph so that some, renumbered with the publishing house's history as a driving force, would be repositioned toward the top of the summary. The writer did the renumbering, stopping occasionally to ask himself questions like, "I wonder if I should begin a new paragraph here." Painstakingly (the session lasted thirty-five minutes), tutor and writer hammered out a revised summary that began by stressing the article's main idea. To help the writer close out the summary in a logical, well-organized manner, the tutor suggested that he add a bridge sentence, which eventually began, "Looking back at the long struggle, Chief Executive Officer Bob Clemens said. . . ." For several painful minutes of interaction, the writer had resisted doing anything except simply plopping "In conclusion" in front of the line that began the final paragraph of his original draft.

Voice/Tone Tutorial

Tutors often have to deal with pieces that have inappropriate voice or tone. Voice and tone, and the persona they create in a piece of writing, is something that many writers have very narrow experience with. A writer in an office, for example, may know only the "voice from above" in the memo in which the boss tells underlings what to do. A high school student may know only the phony inflated "college" voice that one composition theorist calls "Engfish" (Macrorie 1970). Inexperienced writers may know only the voices they have experience with, the casual voices of everyday life. Any writer with such narrow experience is likely to use an inappropriate voice as soon as the rhetorical situation calls for a voice that's a half-step beyond the ones they know.

We train tutors to help writers hear and correct inappropriate voice or tone by showing them two scholars' views of voice and four strategies that can bring writers to a greater awareness of the voice in their piece. When they sense that voice/tone is the area most in need of improvement, the tutors can then quickly "teach" the nature of voice in writing using the two views and one of the four strategies to help the writer see what voice is dominant in the piece. The tutor then discusses the writer's audience and purpose for the piece.

Tutor Questions

- Is the voice you hear in the piece the one you expect to hear, given the audience and purpose of your piece?
- What kind of clothes is the person you created wearing, and do they seem appropriate?
- Is the piece the right mix of tough, sweet, and stuffy; formal, consultative, and casual?

Strategies

- *Voice: tough, sweet, and stuffy.* The first of the two ways we teach tutors to explain voice in writing uses Walker Gibson's (1966) studies of American prose style. He categorizes American prose as being a mixture of just three different types of styles—tough, sweet, and stuffy.

> *Tough* style is the voice of a hard person who has been around, who is worldly-wise and experienced—a person like Hemingway, Bogart, or certain sports writers. The language is simple and direct. Strong feelings are concealed behind a manner that is curt, quick, and to the point.

> *Sweet* style is the style of advertising. The persona speaks directly and informally to the reader as a particular person, often addressing the reader as "you." The intention is to secure intimacy, and the language is ingeniously contrived—sometimes to the point of stylized exaggeration—to build a bridge of warmth and closeness with the reader (for example, in Toyota's "I love what you do for me!" and Microsoft's "Where do you want to go today?").

> *Stuffy* style is the language of bureaucracy, officialdom, and some professions, often written in the voice of the organization or group. It is inflated and refuses to assume a personal connection. Legislation, contracts, research proposals, and some scholarly journals are written in stuffy style.

These three—tough, sweet, and stuffy—are mixed to form the voice of contemporary American prose. Sometimes one is used exclusively or predominates, but more often all are present to varying degrees.

- *Voice: formal, consultative, and casual.* The second view of voice we teach tutors is Martin Joos' (1961) ideas about levels of formality in modern English. Joos lays out a five-part spectrum of levels. Tutors rarely encounter the levels at the two extremes—*frozen* language, the language of law and contracts; and *intimate* language, the language of love letters. We concentrate on the center three: formal, consultative, and casual.

> *Formal* voice is the voice of a research report in a professional journal. Its purpose is to inform a distant audience about technical or specialized information.

> *Consultative* voice is the level at which the work of the world gets done. Its purpose is to inform, but it distances the reader less than formal voice does, perhaps even helping the reader understand the general background of an issue. Consultative voice is the voice of the policy statement and the office memo.

> *Casual* voice is the level for friends and insiders. It is the voice of a personal letter or an e-mail to an office buddy. It assumes that the writer and reader share much in the way of knowledge and experience.

Applying Joos' view lets tutors both see and describe the mixtures of voice that make up the level of formality in a specific piece. A mixture of two or even three levels is common.

Read aloud. Though they may not have experience with voice in writing, writers typically have an experienced—even sophisticated—ear for voice in speech. To help the writer "hear" the voice in a piece, ask her to read aloud at regular speaking volume. Then ask her to describe the voice heard and evaluate its appropriateness to the given audience and purpose. Some writers aren't comfortable reading aloud; if that seems to be the case with your writer, offer to read aloud yourself.

Audience and/or purpose analysis. To begin to deal indirectly with issue of voice, first deal with audience and purpose to get a sense of what voice would be appropriate for the piece. Many rhetoric handbooks describe sophisticated analysis schemes. Audience can be analyzed for such concerns as values, power relationship, personal closeness to the writer, current knowledge of the topic, and expectations for pieces like the present one. Purpose can be analyzed for such traditional rhetorical concerns as persuasion, explanation, reaction, justification, and personal connection. Once the writer understands the piece's audience and purpose, he can often describe what voice would be appropriate.

Metaphors and analogies. Ask the writer for metaphors or analogies for the voice or level of formality she thinks appropriate to the piece's audience and purpose. Use questions like these:

- If someone were speaking in this voice, how would they dress?
- What music would they listen to?
- What would their facial expression be like?
- What would they order for dinner?
- What car would they drive?

Ask the writer to draw a picture or find a photo that depicts the appropriate persona or the present voice in the piece.

Role-play. Many of the pieces you'll work with will have a defined and specific audience. Use role-playing to bring that audience to the foreground. Ask the writer about the audience to help him clarify its salient characteristics. Then ask the writer to role-play one member of the potential audience while you role-play another. For example, to role-play how a boss might react to a memo, ask the writer about the boss, then ask him to play the boss while you play a higher-level boss. This kind of role-playing often helps the writer discover the appropriate level of formality.

Example of voice/tone tutorial. In one tutorial, a first-year college student said flat out that he wrote a paper to show his English teacher what a good writer he was. He described a weekend at a state park with statements like these:

> It permits the exstacy of highly related emotions and values to be contemplated through your retrieval of mediated thought. . . . Given quitesome times, you seem to contemplate and interpret your own intuitions.

The tutor asked the student to read the piece aloud in a regular speaking voice. After about four sentences, the student chuckled and the tutor asked why. The student said, "Nobody writes like that . . . except in English class." With further discussion, the student reported that this was the type of writing that always got him an A in AP English in high school. The tutor then explained the two theories of voice and asked the student to decide which type of voice in each theory seemed best for the piece. The writer chose "tough with some sweet" and "consultative but on the casual side," shook his head with a chuckle, and set off to rewrite.

An art history major brought her first paper from the first course she took for her major to a writing center tutor. She was concerned about whether or not "it sounded smart enough . . . like a major should write." The tutor explained the two theories of voice, and the student decided that the assignment, to analyze a painting, was best done "tough and stuffy about equal" and "consultative with a little formal." She had written sentences like these:

> Penetrating from top to bottom, filling the picture to the middle, they [elements of perspective] create a recessional movement which affects even the placement of mass and color. . . . Contrast of color and recession of space, therefore, create the subject matter and the theme of the painting.

In the discussion that followed, tutor and writer agreed that the piece generally hit the appropriate tough/stuffy and consultative/formal balance. The writer left the tutorial feeling that she had indeed entered the discourse community of art history majors.

Lower Order Concerns

Lower order concerns (LOCs), which are vital to preparing any finished piece, are matters related to surface appearance, correctness, and standard rules of written English. It makes sense for tutors and writers to shift attention to these matters once HOCs have been addressed. Tutors must have a sense of what's important to work on, since it would be a disservice to simply help a writer clean up a handful of errors in a draft that is otherwise devoid of ideas, leaving a paper that is technically correct but lacking in substance.

When you judge that it is time to zero in on LOCs, usually later in the process of writing a piece, look at the sentence structure and mechanics of the draft. Pose these questions and recommend appropriate strategies:

Direct Statement Tutorial

Tutor Question

▪ Have you used the subject-verb-object (S-V-O) sentence where possible, thus avoiding the wordiness of passive voice and the sentence beginning "there is," "there are," and so on?

Strategy

▪ *Nouns into verbs.* Help the writer look for words that are in noun form but could be transformed into verb form. These words often end in "-ment" or "-tion." By changing "reduction" to "reduce," for example, you can make a statement leaner and more direct.

Sentence Combining Tutorial

Tutor Question

- Are there sentences that can be combined?

Strategies

- *Key words.* If you notice that a writer has a tendency to string short, choppy sentences together in a way that creates an immature style, help him identify key words in each statement that can be incorporated into slightly longer, fuller sentences.

- *Reshuffle.* If a writer seems locked into a dominant sentence pattern (for example, sentences frequently begin with a dependent clause), suggest that she reshuffle the sentences. Options for combining sentences, embedding information, and achieving sentence pattern variety include using relative clauses, noun substitutes, subordination, coordination, appositives, participles, prepositional phrases, and absolutes.

- *Creative nonfiction.* Refer the student to a work of a creative nonfiction writer such as John McPhee, Joan Didion, or Frank McCourt. Virtually any page of such a writer's work will put the student in touch with artfully wrought sentences that vary in length and style. In a single page or even a paragraph, McPhee and others conduct a virtual clinic on how to skillfully employ the repertoire of sentence types available.

Wordiness Tutorial

Tutor Question

- Can you eliminate unnecessary words?

Strategies

- *Adverbs.* It is arbitrary, but rewarding, to recommend that the writer search for and delete all adverbs ("basically," "virtually," "surprisingly," "really"), then later restore the ones that are indispensable to enhancing description.

- *Fillers.* Help the writer weed out the extra words that are typically found in conversation ("you know," "well," "now").

- *Doubles.* Help the writer delete doubled words ("each and every," "first and foremost").

▪ *Redundant modifiers.* Help the writer drop redundant modifiers ("*future* plans," "*final* outcome").

▪ *Redundant categories.* Help the writer eliminate redundant categories ("period of time," "large in size," "pink in color").

Cohesion Tutorial

Tutor Question

▪ Is the movement from sentence to sentence clear?

Strategy

▪ *Establish connections.* Help the writer determine if there is a sense of cohesion or connectedness as sentences are spun out one after the other. Look for verbal cues (transitional words) or graphic cues (headings, underlinings that reinforce points being made) that help build bridges and establish ties between the information in once sentence and the information introduced in the next one.

Spelling Tutorial

Tutor Question

▪ What types of spelling errors did you make?

Strategies

▪ *Reference tools.* Urge the writer to use spelling-checker software, which, although fallible, can be helpful and time-saving. Or show the writer how to use a spelling dictionary, which lets a reader locate the proper spelling of a word in seconds.

▪ *Word logs.* Recommend that the writer keep a personalized log of her most commonly misspelled words to refer to.

▪ *Simplified rules.* Look for common sources of spelling errors (such as diphthongs—"ie" and "ei"), then simplify which spelling rules the writer needs to memorize.

▪ *Pronunciation.* Help the writer with spelling errors that stem from pronunciation by alerting him to differences between his pronunciation and the pronunciation dictated by the standard spelling.

Fragments Tutorial

Tutor Question

▪ Are sentence boundaries correctly marked?

Strategies

- *Tag questions, yes-no questions, embedding.* Teach writers to use the *tag questions, yes-no questions,* and *embedding operations* invented by Rei Noguchi (1991) to detect and correct fragments. Here's how each operation would use this sentence from Seymour Hersh's "On the Nuclear Edge," from the March 29, 1993, *New Yorker*:

> Pakistan was rewarded for its support with large amounts of American military and economic aid.

The idea is to show the writer how to test a potentially problematic sentence to determine whether or not it has a subject (a sentence fragment lacks a subject).

> *Tag question:* Pakistan was rewarded for its support by large amounts of American military and economic aid, weren't they? (The pronoun at the end of the tag question refers to the subject of the sentence—or identifies the lack of a subject.)
>
> *Yes-no question:* Was Pakistan rewarded for its support by large amounts of military and economic aid? (The "helping" verb has been moved; the subject is the first noun to the immediate right of the moved auxiliary verb.)
>
> *Embedding:* They refused to believe that Pakistan was rewarded for its support by large amounts of military and economic aid. (Use embedding to identify sentences [or fragment errors] by opening the sentence with "They refused to believe the idea that." Our example would pass this test as a sentence.)

- *"To" and "-ing" words.* When "to" or an "-ing" word appears at or near the start of a word group, a fragment may result. For example:

> Larry walked all over the neighborhood yesterday. Trying to find his dog Bo.

> At the expensive restaurant, John used his napkin. To impress his date.

An "-ing" or "to" fragment can often be corrected by attaching the fragment to the sentence that comes before or after it.

Comma Splice and Run-on Tutorial

Tutor Question

- Do some of the sentences seem to be fused or rushing forward?

Strategies

- *Pronouns.* A comma splice (improperly using a comma to connect sentences) or run-on sentence (fusing two sentences together with no punctuation to signal the end of one and the beginning of the other) often occurs when the second independent clause begins with a pronoun. Teach the writer to look for such instances and change the punctuation to correct them.

> *Wrong:* Mark McGwire is a power hitter, he set the major league record for home runs in one season.

> *Correct:* Mark McGwire is a power hitter. He set the major league record for home runs in one season.

▪ *Transition words.*   Another leading cause of comma splices and run-ons is when the second independent clause begins with a conjunctive adverb or other transition word.

> *Wrong:* Mark McGwire is a power hitter, however, he had never come close to hitting seventy homers before.

> *Correct:* Mark McGwire is a power hitter. However, he had never come close to hitting seventy homers before.

▪ *Misplaced examples.*   Comma splices and run-ons often occur when the second independent clause explains or gives an example of the information in the first independent clause.

> *Wrong:* Mark McGwire has had many productive baseball seasons, the summer of 1998 was his most spectacular so far.

> *Correct:* Mark McGwire has had many productive baseball seasons. The summer of 1998 was his most spectacular so far.

Verb Agreement Tutorial

Tutor Question
▪ When your subject says "one," does your verb say "one" too?

Strategy

▪ *De Beaugrande's approach.*   Muriel Harris (1986) summarizes Robert de Beaugrande's approach for helping writers first find the verb in a sentence this way:

> 1. Insert a "denial word" into a statement (doesn't/don't, didn't/won't).
> 2. The "agreeing verb" of the original statement is the one located after the denial word.

> Example: Our boss wants to call a meeting.
>   Our boss doesn't want to call a meeting.

(This is especially helpful for students who wonder whether "want" or "call" may be the verb here.) (127)

Verb Tense Tutorial

Tutor Question

- Does your piece say "today," "yesterday," or "tomorrow" consistently throughout?

Strategy

- *Today, yesterday, tomorrow.* If a writer is bothered by inconsistent verb tense, ask him to read through his pieces and stop at each sentence boundary to check whether it is in present, past, or future tense, saying the word "today," "yesterday," or "tomorrow" aloud.

General Proofreading Tutorial

Tutor Question

- Have you tried other "finishing up" strategies?

Strategies

- *Online assistance.* Recommend that the writer consult online writing labs (OWLs) for online writing handbooks or grammar hotlines (see the "Electronic Resources" section at the back of the book).

- *Line screen.* A big challenge in helping writers proofread their own text is making sure they stay on task and don't get sidetracked by reading for content. One way to do this is to have the writer use a line screen, or even just a ruler, to view only one line at a time. This makes reading tough, but improves proofreading.

- *Sentence sequence.* Tell the writer to read the piece backward, sentence by sentence, to catch spelling errors and omissions. Reading sentences out of sequence will let the writer concentrate on individual words.

- *Page sequence.* Encourage the writer to read pages out of order. This is another way of taking words and ideas out of their original context, which enables the writer/proofreader to review each page as a discrete unit.

- *Cluster.* Remind the writer that mistakes tend to cluster; if she finds one typographical error, she should look carefully nearby for others.

- *Read aloud.* Have the writer read the piece aloud to himself. Hearing his own words often lets a writer catch incongruous word combinations or words or word endings that he has inadvertently omitted.

- *Hard copy.* If you're tutoring a writer at a computer terminal, recommend that the writer print out a hard copy of the piece to proofread, rather than proofreading on-screen.

Responding to the Whole Piece of Writing

Both when working face-to-face with a writer and when face-to-face interaction isn't an option, tutors sometimes need to step back from micromanaging HOCs and LOCs and respond to a piece of writing as a whole, first viewing it from an overall impressionistic perspective, then responding to the writing and the writer holistically.

Giving Feedback in Person

One simple holistic feedback technique is for the tutor to ask the writer to submit a draft along with a paragraph describing what she tried to accomplish (Wiggins 1993). After reading the draft, the tutor tells the writer whether the draft's effect matches the writer's intent, and points out one place in the draft where he lost interest in the piece.

Tom Romano (1987) outlines a three-step method for tutors to use when responding to the overall effectiveness of a piece. First the tutor reads the entire draft and describes two strong parts to the writer. Next the tutor quotes the most effective sentence in the piece. Then the tutor identifies one spot in the draft that needs to be clarified and poses one question about it to the writer.

Another method that allow tutors to focus on the whole draft is a "stuttered" response, which gives the writer information about how strongly the lead relates to the piece and if it reflects what she intended it to. The tutor reads only the lead (the first line, first paragraph, or first two paragraphs), then stops to let the writer know her reaction to these three questions:

- What words or phrases struck me the most?
- What has this section said so far?
- What do I now expect the rest of the paper to say?

The tutor then reads the remainder of the piece and gives the writer general responses about the whole text.

Giving Feedback on Paper

Tutors sometimes need to tend to a piece in a writer's absence, perhaps because a draft is available before a scheduled tutorial session. Tutors can give feedback on paper by writing comments on the draft or by filling out a rating sheet.

Writing comments on the draft. Comments jotted on the draft can serve as guideposts for the tutorial conversation, if there will be one, and give the writer something to refer to later on. It is important that the tutor frame written comments in a way that lets the writer learn from them. There are both general and specific strategies for writing effective comments.

General Strategies for Writing Comments

1. Use the priority of concerns to guide your written response (HOCs to LOCs). Present comments so the writer knows which problems with text are most important and which are of lesser importance. Especially at first, refrain from checkmarking, circling, or underlining grammatical errors.

2. Use comments primarily to call attention to a particular strength or weakness in the piece—one that can be located precisely at the point where it occurs.

3. Studies reveal that hostile, mean-spirited written comments are counterproductive or go unread. Frame your comments so that you are not taking the writer's attention away from her purposes and focusing attention on your own thinking.

4. Don't feel obligated to do all the "fixing." If you notice one pervasive flaw, say with spelling, jot a note to the writer that you found six spelling miscues and let him identify and correct them.

5. Write comments that are text-specific, uniquely aimed at that writer and that paper, rather than vague, rubber-stamped remarks.

Specific Strategies for Writing Comments

1. Pose at least two questions that ask for clarification or that seek other possible views or more information on the subject.

2. Avoid using marginal shorthand like "?" and "What?" and "So what?" and "Be specific!" and "AWK." Don't leave the writer guessing. It's better to write a few fully explained comments than to flood a piece with cryptic jottings.

3. Let the writer know what specific lines, ideas, and stylistic touches you find pleasing or that you recognize as representing the writer's progress.

4. Make a personal connection at least once on every draft by using the writer's name or initials.

5. When you make a specific, concrete suggestion for improvement, try couching it in a qualifier: "You might try . . ." or "Why don't you add . . ." or "Another way of writing the lead might be. . ."

6. Use a pen or marker that stands out from the writer's printed text—and avoid red ink.

7. Phrase your comments in a way that invites the writer to write more. Don't be sarcastic or terse.

8. If you notice a pattern of errors or a problem area that emerges throughout the piece, comment on it in a global way at the end of the piece.

Using a rating sheet. Another way a tutor can provide written feedback about a draft is by filling out a sheet that rates the draft in several areas. (See Figure 6–1.) After reading the draft, circle the number that indicates the writer's level of performance in each area, pinpointing the draft's strengths and weak spots. Here is a rating sheet that covers nine areas of HOCs and LOCs. (This sheet is somewhat similar to the one recommended in Chapter 7 for peer writing teams to use when tutoring in the workplace—see Figure 7–1.)

Summary

We'll wrap up this chapter with a summary of our writing tutorial model, with scenarios, question sets, and strategies listed in a barebones way. This model is not intended to be a recipe for tutors to follow lockstep. In fact, we can't imagine a tutorial session that would require the tutor to adhere to the full model. Rather, we ask that tutors be mindful of the uniqueness of each tutorial encounter, keep to the basic situation (no topic, topic but no draft, draft), and work on a hierarchy of HOCs to LOCs by using the questions and strategies that seem most appropriate.

Our Tutoring Model

Every Session

Questions and Procedures

- Get acquainted
- Find out what the assignment is, whether the writer understands it fully, and when it is due. Determine what kind of writing it is

Figure 6–1
Rating Sheet for Responding to Drafts

Rating Sheet for Responding to Drafts

Writer _____ Tutor/Reader _____

4 Distinguished; 3 Proficient; 2 Apprentice; 1 Novice

1. Title. Provides a forecasting or intriguing clue	4	3	2	1
2. Lead. First few lines capture the reader in three seconds, perhaps innovatively	4	3	2	1
3. Focus. The piece says just one thing	4	3	2	1
4. Information. Writer presents specific, accurate bits of informa- tion and details	4	3	2	1
5. Order. The piece has a shape that has bridges between paragraphs and that moves the piece forward	4	3	2	1
6. Voice. The piece shows evidence of a distinctive persona and/or appropriate tone	4	3	2	1
7. Ending. The piece offers a satisfy- ing sense of closure	4	3	2	1
8. Grammar/Usage/Mechanics. The piece shows control over grammar, spelling, and punctuation	4	3	2	1
9. Risk Taking. The piece shows work beyond the writer's comfort level	4	3	2	1

(explanatory, expressive, persuasive, an abstract, a resume, etc.), the intended audience, and the voice required by asking these questions:

> What are you trying to do in this paper?
>
> Are you writing to someone other than your instructor/supervisor/parent?
>
> What kind of writer's voice do you think is most appropriate for the piece (friendly and intimate, distant and unsociable, etc.)?

- Find out what approach the writer is already using or plans to use for the assignment.

When the Writer Needs Help Finding a Topic

- Explore with the writer how to discover a worthwhile topic by asking these questions:

> What have you been thinking or reading about lately?
> What are you curious to know more about?

- Use these strategies:
    writing territories
    free writing
    rapid sketches
    conversation
    free talking
    doodling
    three-by-five card focusing drill
    the alert writer

When the Writer Has a Topic, but No Draft

- Explore with the writer how she might go about gathering or producing ideas and materials about the topic by asking these questions:

> What do you know about the subject?
>
> What don't you know about the subject?
>
> How can you look for connections among the tidbits you already know that might suggest new directions?

- Use these strategies:
    cubing
    twenty questions
    particle/wave/field
    pentad
    looping

titles
clustering
point-of-view mapping

When the Writer Has a Rough Draft

- Sit next to the writer and read along silently as he reads the page aloud. Encourage him to tell you what he wants the two of you to look and listen for. Ask the following questions:

  What works best in your piece?
  What do you like best or feel most satisfied about?
  What works least in the piece?
  Which parts did you have trouble writing?
  Which parts don't feel right?

- Stop whenever you wish to explore alternatives with the writer. Give him every chance to solve a problem before you offer specific solutions. Your task is to help the writer see the problem and solve it. Avoid jumping in and writing out the solution yourself. Ask questions and use strategies that let the writer do the writing:

For HOCs

Questions About Thesis/Focus

What's the central issue of the piece?

What's the dominant statement you want your piece to make?

When the reader is finished reading, what do you want him to walk away with?

If your roommate, colleague, or sibling walked up to you and said, "What are you writing about?" what would you say?

Strategies

one-sentence summary
nutshelling and teaching
talk aloud
make a promise
create a headline or bumper sticker

Questions About Development

Can you tell me more?

Point to places where you think a reader might want you to tell more.

If you read this aloud to a few readers, what do you think their first questions would be?

If black were the color of the parts with lots of information, gray the color of those with less information, and white those with even less information, what color would this part of your piece be?

Strategies

focused free writing
oral composition
mapping
matrices
playing your thoughts

Questions About Structure/Organization

How did you tie each part and subpart to the thesis/focus?

What do you think a reader would see as the major parts of your piece?

Do you think the piece could be significantly improved by reordering the major parts or the subparts in a specific section?

Do you think the piece could be improved by making the divisions between parts more noticeable to the reader?

Strategies

just talk about it
skeleton
tree diagram
coloring
outlining
transitions

Questions About Voice/Tone

Is the voice in the piece the one you expect to hear given the audience and purpose of the piece?

What kind of clothes is the persona you created wearing, and do they seem appropriate?

Is the piece the right mix of tough, sweet, stuffy, formal, consultative, and casual?

Strategies

tough/sweet/stuffy
formal/consultative/casual
read aloud
audience/purpose analysis

metaphors and analogies
role-play

For LOCs

Questions

Have you used the subject-verb-object sentence?

Are there sentences that can be combined?

Can you eliminate unnecessary words?

Is the movement from sentence to sentence clear?

What types of spelling errors did you make?

Are the sentence boundaries correctly marked?

Do some of the sentences seem to be fused or rushing forward?

When your subject says "one," does your verb say "one," too?

Does your piece say "today," "yesterday," and "tomorrow" consistently throughout?

Have you tried other "finishing up" strategies?

At the end of the tutorial session, if it seems appropriate, recommend self-help materials to the writer and invite her back for another visit soon. If the session took place in a writing center, do the necessary record keeping.

Chapter Seven

Tutoring in Different Places

Writing tutorials don't always take place where you would expect to find them. There are settings other than traditional writing classrooms or school writing centers in which one-to-one writing meetings can flourish. One of us recently donned a hard hat in order to enter the premises of the Outokumpu American Brass manufacturing plant to conduct a three-day basic writing skills workshop for middle managers. Part of the workshop involved training the workers to be skilled and trusted readers as they respond to their colleagues' on-the-job drafts. Donald Murray (1979a) reports having writing conferences with students at his home, over the telephone, or at lunch in a campus cafeteria. He has conducted casual tutorials when he sees students at hockey games, at the store, or even passing on the sidewalk. A student will say, "Hey, I tried to lead this way," or "Will you look at this?" or "What do you think about that?" As a writing tutor, Murray is always on call and engaged in dialogue with writers who need assistance. Nancie Atwell (1998) also describes having writing conferences "on the run" as she bumps into students in the stairwell at school. Within reason, there are virtually no unorthodox or inappropriate places to hold a writing tutorial; an open-minded, accessible tutor will seize any opportunity.

Teachers face an ever-increasing emphasis on high standards and are often asked to share our expertise to help writers in the community. We find ourselves donning hard hats literally and figuratively, training workers on the job to act as peer writing tutors or speaking to parent-teacher organizations to prepare parents to tutor their children at home as a supplement to the classroom or as part of a home schooling program. This chapter discusses how to tutor writers in three special contexts: writing across the curriculum, in the workplace, and at home.

Tutoring Across the Curriculum

Much of the writing that students do is in courses other than English. It is wise, then, for tutors to be prepared to help students deal with writing for courses across the disciplines. Tutors are regularly asked to assist writers who are working on lab reports, research papers, analytical essays, business proposals, opinion papers, reviews, and so on.

The question of how to tutor students in a realm of writing that is wider than the usual English-course personal narratives and personal essays is under debate. The debate deals with three features of the tutoring process:

the tutor's role

the tutor's qualifications

the place tutoring occurs

This section explains each of these features and discusses strategies for tutoring across the disciplines successfully. We believe that there is no right or wrong answer in this debate, but that tutors need to have a variety of useful strategies and understandings that they can apply as they tutor across the curriculum.

The Tutor's Role

Should the writing tutor function as tutor, teacher, or both? We believe that in most situations the tutor should be somewhere between teacher and student; should be trained in assisting writers and supporting the writing process. Therefore, the tutor should be someone who knows more about tutoring, teaching, learning, and writing than most of the writers seeking tutoring do. But the tutor is not the teacher in knowledge, power, or experience. The tutor typically stands between teacher and writer, creating in the tutorial a collaborative atmosphere that lets students take risks they wouldn't attempt in the more charged atmosphere of a classroom. In effect, the tutor creates a new institutional space for learning, what Muriel Harris (1992) calls "a middle world" and which John Trimbur (1983) values because this middle world is less constrained by cultural and institutional politics than classrooms and campuses, creating what Louise Smith (1986) sees as "loci of specialized authority."

When tutoring occurs across disciplines, the tutor may take on more teacherly characteristics. In some across-the-curriculum tutoring designs, the tutor is a peer who is knowledgeable about course content. Writers regularly ask both writing and content questions of tutors when they know that the tutor is knowledgeable about the content of the course. This can happen anytime in tutoring, no matter what the tutor's background is, but in across-the-curriculum situations, content questions are a regular part of the tutoring process.

Tutors always guard against being "little teachers," but when they work with writers from across the curriculum—especially if the writers know that the tutor has content-area expertise—the tutor moves from the traditional role of the middle-grounder toward the role of teacher. Mary Soliday (1995) found that the best tutoring occurs when tutors connect with writing across the curriculum programs and therefore take on some teacherly characteristics.

The Tutor's Qualifications

Does a tutor need just general knowledge of writing and tutoring, or additional specialized knowledge about the content and forms of specific disciplines? Susan Hubbuch (1988) believes that a tutor doesn't need specialized knowledge. She argues that the very lack of knowledge may be an advantage, allowing a tutor to see text as a reader rather than as an expert. And Tori Haring-Smith (1992), in promoting her popular Writing Fellows program, sees the stance of educated lay reader as the most beneficial for tutors across the curriculum. Generalist tutors, she argues, can more readily see when a writer is confused about what she is trying to say because they are less likely to fill gaps with disciplinary knowledge.

However, Jean Kiedaisch and Sue Dinitz (1993), who studied tutoring sessions with generalist tutors and discipline-specific tutors, argue that the generalist tutor has limitations when working across the curriculum. They report that:

> The only tutors who worked successfully on the global level were knowledgeable tutors . . . the tutor's knowledge of how to think and write in the discipline did seem important. Good tutoring strategies were not enough . . . students writing papers for upper-level courses would be best served by carefully trained tutors with knowledge of the discipline. (69, 72)

Kiedaisch and Dinitz suggest either recruiting tutors from across the curriculum so that a variety of majors are available across the pool of tutors or, following Linda Scanlon (1986), turning generalist tutors into specialists by having tutor training workshops given by faculty who are interested in writing in their disciplines.

Kiedaisch and Dinitz do recognize two problems with tutors working with students in their same discipline. First, knowledgeable tutors have to be particularly cautious about taking a too authoritative stance and appropriating the piece of writing; ownership of the piece is the writer's and must remain so for the greatest growth in writing and revision proficiency to occur. Second, knowledgeable tutors take on a much larger burden than generalists tutors do because they have to not only help the writer improve *this* piece and *this* writing process, but also to teach the conventions of the particular discipline, which should be the responsibility of the department sponsoring the course and the major.

We believe that well-trained tutors can be of significant help to writers in any course, but that well-trained tutors who are knowledgeable about a discipline can be of even more help because they can read like the audience for the piece, in this case experts in the discipline. One possible compromise in the debate would be to think of the specialist as being not too specialized. If a writing tutor is a physics major, her expertise in the conventions of physics would make her a better reader of chemistry, math, economics, business statistics, and scientific sociology.

Perhaps the best would be to acknowledge areas of expertise among all tutors and cluster that expertise into specialty teams based on academic areas. Tutoring teams might be organized like the colleges in a university: science, humanities, business, education. Our physics major could be a member of a scientific team that dealt primarily with writers from science, technology, and related scientific stances in other disciplines. An English major might be a member of a humanities team, which would tutor writers not just from the traditional humanities but from across the disciplines when those disciplines take a humanistic stance (for example, when a student is assigned to write a portrait of a famous scientist, a profile of a patient in abnormal psychology, an ethnography of an urban street gang, a persuasive sales letter in marketing, or a history of the cathode ray tube in electrical engineering). Tutors would work with writers not by the course the writer was taking, but by the type of writing the writer was assigned in that course. The English 101 student who is writing an analysis of advertising for that course could profit from a business team tutor as much as, maybe even more than, from a humanities tutor.

The Place Tutoring Occurs

Writing across the curriculum programs can interact with tutors who are stationed at the writing center, where students from classes across the curriculum go for tutoring. Harris (1992) outlines many of the advantages of this design:

- There is a place where tutoring is available most of the day.
- The writing center has readily available resources to support the tutor—other tutors, the director, printed references, and word processing, desktop publishing, and presentation software.
- The student can see that she is not alone in her concerns about a writing assignment because the writing center is filled with writers and tutors working collaboratively.
- The student can see the importance of writing, and the institutional commitment to it, by the site and staff that have been committed to improving writing.

Others point out some of the disadvantages of centralized tutoring in a writing across the curriculum program. Tutors who work out of a writing center often don't have the necessary understanding about the discipline-specific writing that writers are struggling to learn. Tutors have little understanding of the writing assignments and how they figure as part of the organized experience of learning content and skills or as part of the interaction between teacher and student. As Smith (1986) reminds us, tutors "cannot possibly know the contexts of assigned readings and class discussions in which various writing assignments are to be prepared. The result is an inevitable tension between the authority of teachers and that of the writing center." (4) Too often tutors hear "but that's the way the teacher wants it" or "we always do it like that in my major" from writers working on across-the-curriculum projects.

Many institutions have designed across-the-curriculum tutoring programs that try to incorporate the advantages and reduce the disadvantages of centralizing tutoring at a writing center. Harris (1992) reports on a variety of strategies that allows tutors to be associated with writing centers but also to be closely connected to classes across the disciplines. Each tutor is attached to one to three sections of a class, perhaps an English department writing class, an introductory general education class, or a class for majors in a specific discipline. The tutor meets with the teacher for an initial interview about the writing goals and forms in the course. Often the tutor attends several class meetings to get a sense of the academic and emotional environment; she also meets regularly with the teacher. The tutor often tutors during class or at scheduled hours in or near the teacher's office. This close relationship between teacher and tutor requires almost constant negotiation of the role of the tutor, which can range from outside class helper to in-class assistant teacher—whatever makes teacher and tutor comfortable.

Soliday (1995) studied this curriculum-based tutoring strategy, labeling a tutor who worked almost exclusively at the writing center an "outsider" and one who did all tutoring in the classroom an "insider." Although Soliday attached her tutors only to composition courses, what she found seems applicable to attaching tutors to courses across the disciplines: Successful tutors are a true hybrid of insider and outsider. Insider/outsider (I/O) tutors reported that they had more confidence in their tutoring because they knew the students as writers and people and because they knew the teacher's assignments and expectations. They also reported that they had more authority as trusted readers because students were aware that the tutors knew the class and the professor. Finally, I/O tutors reported being better able to identify the social dynamic between professors and students. This showed tutors that students were learning not only how to write, but also how to adjust to the individual teacher and the curriculum.

In the composition classes Soliday looked at, tutors spent time in the following ways:

- Conferences with students during writing workshops
- "Takes student out" during class for short conference
- Discusses assignments with teacher during office hours
- Circulates during class and works with small groups
- Leads mini-workshops during class
- Teaches one or two classes during the course
- Announces her hours at the writing center
- Conferences with students at the writing center
- After early regular attendance at class, tutor gradually withdraws to work mostly at the writing center (65)

By extrapolating from Soliday's research, we can arrive at some suggestions for tutors who are attached to classes across the disciplines. As Soliday rightly emphasizes,

> The tutor's role—and perhaps the teacher's to a certain extent—shifted because in order to establish the tutor's authority, . . . tutors and teachers had to contextualize tutor's roles for the students in the class. (67)

This contextualization was accomplished by collaboration between tutor and teacher through these strategies:

- The tutor introduced herself to the class.

- The tutor was named on the syllabus or course description.
- The tutor was active during class.
- The tutor decided with the teacher what her role would be.
- Conferencing occurred during class.
- Teachers took the class to the writing center for an introduction.
- Some teachers asked students to keep tutoring session reports.
- During class discussions teachers asked tutors for their opinions, especially when dealing with writing assignments. (67)

Not all of these things will happen in every course, but using one or more will help teacher and tutor connect and interact in ways that lead to productive integration of tutoring, writing centers, and classes across the curriculum. Overall, the process for I/O tutors, whether in composition classes or classes across the disciplines, is to immerse themselves in the culture and language of the classroom until tutor and teacher feel that the tutor has a true insider's perspective; then the tutor withdraws to the writing center and uses its advantages for tutoring during the rest of the course.

Even when tutors working across the disciplines strike the right balance to be I/O tutors, they can do still more to ensure profitable interactions with writing-across-the-curriculum programs and faculty:

- Tutors, even in designs that do not directly attach tutors to courses, can interview faculty in various disciplines to study the required forms of writing, get model assignments from previous classes, and collect information on what constitutes quality writing and successful completion of assignments.

- Tutors can hold orientation meetings with faculty to explain the process and complexity of tutoring and teaching writing one-to-one, along with preparing faculty from the disciplines to join with instructors who have an attached tutor, or at least to take advantage of the writing center for their students.

- Tutors can run regular workshops for faculty across the disciplines on such topics as designing writing assignments, using peer response groups in and out of class, incorporating writing assignments into courses, using short write-to-learn activities, using journals and learning logs, and teaching ESL students.

- Tutors can act as consultants to departments and programs that want to increase the portion of their curriculum that's devoted to writing.

- Tutors can start a regular writing workshop that uses tutoring and peer response groups to help faculty members become more comfortable writers. Instructors who feel at home with writing are more likely to assign it in classes and to join an across-the-curriculum writing and tutoring project.

Tutors working across the disciplines might suggest some of these short write-to-learn activities to writers in various subject areas:

- Speculative writing: At the beginning of a class or lecture, students write without stopping for three or four minutes about the day's topic.

- The one-minute essay: Whether students are attending a lab, lecture, or discussion, they write for a minute at the end of each class about what they learned that day and about what questions they still have.

- The learning log: Writers keep a log of informal notes and reflections based on readings and lectures from the content-area course. A log helps writers think, organize, ask questions, and work out problems pertaining to writing.

- Graphic organizers: Writers design graphic organizers to help their reading and note-taking. Such graphic guides include topics, main ideas, and essential details.

Tutoring in the Workplace

Our discussions about tutoring writing can also be applied in the workplace, where people continue their development as writers after school and college. Bill McCleary (1998) cites international studies of literacy, sponsored by the Organization for Economic Cooperation and Development (OECD), that recommend improving workplace literacy through on-the-job education. Teachers can provide such instruction, particularly by equipping workers with the response skills of effective writing tutors. According to James Cravens (1997) in the *San Diego Business Journal*, personnel executives report that 25 percent of new hires and 37 percent of current employees lack basic writing competency. Cravens goes on to say that it is no wonder that 35 percent of American companies offer writing training to their staffs. Kenneth Davis (1995) reports that *Training* magazine's 1994 Industry Report found that 54 percent of companies with over 100 employees provided training to improve writing during 1993.

We believe that one of the best kinds of training that teachers can offer companies is to train employees to tutor each other by reading carefully and responding to the memos, letters, and reports generated during the day-to-day routine of the work world.

One form of workplace training that is similar to tutoring is *coaching*. Lin Kroeger (1993) describes the process by which he improved the writing of internal audit reports in his division:

> The coaching process requires timing, location, two-way communication, and restraint. It can occur during the audit, on-site or post-audit, back at the office, depending on the realities of the audit itself. Adequate time must be set aside for the coaching session, and the choice of location for the session should ensure privacy. Then the coach must clearly communicate the diagnosis of the report; converse with the auditor until the auditor can see, understand, and buy into the diagnosis; and then obtain commitment from the auditor to rewrite the document, incorporating the improvements discussed. Throughout, the coach must exercise restraint: avoid writing on the original document; be precise about the flaws while avoiding cruelty; focus on only one or two flaws; be supportive of the auditor's ability to improve; and focus on the criteria for effectiveness not on issues of style. (59)

Kroeger also offered members of his division workshops on concerns ranging from spelling to writing executive summaries, and he regularly brought auditors together in groups of five to eight so he and their peers could give feedback on in-process reports. All in all, Kroeger did many effective things, but, as in so many training ventures in the workplace, Kroeger acted as the one "teacher," with all the auditors as his students. He had writing conferences with each, led small response groups, and gave workshops, but he was the only one who acted in that role.

If Kroeger had trained his auditors to be peer tutors for each other, the effect would have multiplied as all staff got to see themselves as having writing competencies worth sharing with others. Davis (1995) knows the truth of this. He recommends forming "writing teams" whose members act as peer coaches, creating a solid structure on which to build the long-term training needed to improve writing. Davis, however, gives no ideas about how to set up writing teams, structure them in an organization, or schedule sessions during the workday.

Let's consider six types of writing that are commonly required in the workplace and propose questions and focal points that trainers could share when teaching peer tutors how to improve their own and their colleagues' documents.

Memos

Several years ago, when Russ Thomas was the general manager of the National Football League's Detroit Lions and Monte Clark was head coach, their relationship was so strained that they communicated only by written memo. While that arrangement was certainly not ideal, the estranged colleagues were at least aware that the chief function of a memo is as an in-house vehicle to keep fellow employees in touch with company issues.

Memos should be short (Procter and Gamble has set the bar with its legendary one-page memo policy), informal, focused on one topic, orderly, and timely. A peer tutor might respond to a memo draft in these ways:

- After reading only the subject or "re" line, which word strikes you as most important (a memo subject line should be no longer than ten words and should announce the thesis of the memo). With just the subject line in mind, if you were to place this memo in a file folder, how would you label the file?

- Read the rest of the memo draft, then summarize it for the writer. Pretend you have thirty seconds to tell a fellow worker what this memo is all about.

- Identify the memo's strengths.

- Notice whether the writer uses reader-based cues such as lists, underlinings, and short paragraphs.

- Name two things the writer can do to improve the memo draft?

Instructions and Procedural Manuals

Keep it simple. A few years ago, the General Accounting Office found a radar manual that forced technicians to refer to 165 pages in eight documents, looking in forty-one places in those documents, just to repair one particular malfunction. Instructions, directives, and other procedural documents not only need to be simple, they also need to have a clear sense of audience. A peer tutor can help a writer immensely by asking how the reader is supposed to use the information in an instructional document. For example, the tutor might ask if the intended reader is supposed to

- commit the information to memory

- explain the information to someone else at work

- refer to the information while performing a task

- use the information to make a decision

- buy or use a product or service

After helping the writer narrow the purpose of the instructions, the tutor focuses on the draft:

- Look at the title and introduction. Is it clear what process is about to be described, or why the instructions are significant, or how long it will take to complete the steps?

- Check through the document to confirm it uses imperative sentences and such reader-based cues as warnings, cautions, and notes interjected at timely points in the step-by-step narrative.

- Perhaps the best way to help the writer is to test the effectiveness of instructions by walking through them step-by-step to catch ambiguities or omissions.

Proposals

Proposals are persuasive documents that urge readers to support an idea, plan, or project. They can range from one page to hundreds or thousands. Proposals usually identify a problem before suggesting a solution. If you are asked to respond to a colleague's proposal draft, here are some questions to ask:

- Are the ideas that make up the writer's plan clearly presented and backed up by convincing reasons?

- Does the proposal look professional (are there enough visual and verbal reader-friendly cues)?

- Does the proposal come across as something that's worth carrying out?

- What two suggestions might improve this proposal?

- If you were on a panel to approve the proposal in its current form, reject it, or return it for revision, what would you recommend?

Feasibility Reports

A kind of companion, or follow-up, to proposals, feasibility reports study a plan and investigate two questions: "Can it be done?" and "Should it be done?" Feasibility reports usually explore alternative solutions and recommend which option to adopt, based on a careful presentation of data that are matched against criteria. The criteria often cover such concerns as the plan's technological or logistical possibility (Can it be done?); economic practicality (Is it cost-efficient?); ecological soundness (What impact will it have on environment, workplace, home, and community?); and social desirability (Will it help or hurt people?). These questions and criteria can help the peer tutor give useful feedback to the writer of a draft feasibility report. The tutor might ask the following:

- Why is it important for the reader to consider the alternatives?
- Are the criteria reasonable and appropriate?
- Are the facts reliable?
- What are the important features of the alternatives?
- How do the alternatives measure up against the criteria?
- Is there a clear-cut recommendation at the end?

Progress Reports

Progress reports describe the progress of an unfinished project. They might be written quarterly or be related to just one project. They typically have three parts—what's been accomplished so far, what's being done right now, and what still needs to be done before the project is completed. A peer tutor can scan a colleagues' progress report draft and ask questions like these:

- Is it clear whether or not the project is on schedule?
- Is there adequate information in the "work completed so far" segment?
- Does the reader understand what work is currently in progress?
- Is there a thorough explanation of what work needs to be completed?
- Does the writer describe any obstacles or complications that have hindered the project so far or that might hamper future progress (especially toward the end of the project)?
- Is the information presented in chronological order?

Trip Reports

Whether it is about a staff retreat, attendance at a trade show or convention, a troubleshooting or inspection trip, or a site visit, the travel or trip report is an official document—a company record of a work-related trip. Someone who did not make the trip can be an especially effective peer tutor by reading the trip report and describing his reactions in the following ways:

- Tell the writer what you perceive to be the point or focus of the trip report. If you're having trouble discerning one or feel there is more than one, say so.

- Describe as specifically as you can the part or quality of the trip report you like the most.

- Ask questions if you need to. Tell the writer about sections or sentences where you felt slightly confused.

- Tell the writer where you are genuinely interested and want more information, such as more details about events or itinerary, or more information about the writer's overall impression and evaluation.

To address the whole writer at the workplace, peer tutors on writing teams can refer to the rubric shown in Figure 7-1 to guide their feedback about any draft, whether it's of a memo, letter, or report. The response sheet can serve as a discussion point during the tutor's one-to-one talk with the writer and can be used to pinpoint strengths and weaknesses in the document.

Tutoring at Home

This section explains procedures that parents and other caregivers can use when they work as writing tutors with their children. Tutoring in the home has taken on new significance, and it's important for teachers to share these procedures during Parent-Teacher Association meetings or community adult education in-services. Some parents home-school their children, thus becoming the children's primary reader, responder, and tutor. Lines (1997) estimates that as of 1997, from 500,000 to 750,000 students were being homeschooled. Many parents who don't homeschool are taking their job as "helper" more seriously as their children prepare to meet the increasingly rigorous academic standards set by school systems, to gear up for demands of literacy in the workplace, or to successfully compete for college admissions. Parents across the country seem ready to pick up the slack they see in schools that are underfunded and overcrowded; after all, even the best teachers can only do so much. And many schools realize how important the connection between home and school is and have active parental involvement programs for tutoring in school and at home.

Using the home as a site for tutoring is as old as the desire to learn. At-home tutoring is done most often by parents, and sometimes by grandparents, older siblings, or other family members: A father drops into a kitchen chair and helps a child who is struggling with a math problem; a mother checks a piece of writing for mistakes; a sibling who took chemistry last year helps the student understand how to do a lab report; a grandparent helps a child cut out magazine photos for a poster project. Although family members might not call what

Figure 7–1
A Response Sheet for Workplace Drafts

Writer: _____ Date:_____

Peer Tutor/Respondent: _____

4 Excellence Level; 3 Mastery Level; 2 Proficiency Level; 1 Entry Level

1. Purpose. Document says one thing and has a clear goal—to explain, to persuade, or to instruct	4	3	2	1
2. Introduction. The first lines forecast the document's intention	4	3	2	1
3. Style and Tone. Document sounds as if an individual writer is speaking aloud to an individual listene.	4	3	2	1
4. Information. The writer presents specific, accurate pieces of information and details	4	3	2	1
5. Order. Document has a shape which has bridges between paragraphs and which moves the piece forward	4	3	2	1
6. Audience. Document uses visual and verbal cues that make it effectively reader-friendly	4	3	2	1
7. Sentence Fluency. Sentences are clear and of various styles and lengths	4	3	2	1
8. Grammar/Usage/Mechanics. Shows control over grammar, spelling, and punctuation	4	3	2	1

they're doing tutoring, it is exactly that: A one-to-one relationship leads to conversation between a more knowledgeable person and a person who needs assistance in learning. It might be called "helping with homework" or just "helping," but it is tutoring, plain and simple.

Parents might be called the prime tutors since they are the prime sources of oral language use. For the first several years of a child's life, the parent regularly reacts to the child's oral expressions, responding to the meaning the child tries to make and praising the child's growing ability to talk (Wells 1986; Lindfors 1985). Parents are also the first teachers for most children's developing reading and writing as they read stories aloud, take a trip to the library, or encourage the first signature or letter to grandma (Harste, Woodward, and Burke 1984; Baghban 1984; Taylor 1983). Parents are, therefore, successful language and literacy tutors. It seems only reasonable to mobilize them to tutor writing as the child grows. Parents are particularly suited to tutoring because they know so much about the child as person and learner. If a child has a cold, the parent can adjust the tutoring process to fit, offering a slower pace and more encouragement. Or if the child is trying to write dialogue in a story, the parent knows which favorite storybook to grab and use as a model.

If there is a problem with a parent tutoring writing, it often lies with the parent. Many parents will help a child willingly without being asked, but don't feel comfortable thinking of themselves as a "tutor" because they lack teacherly expertise and training. They do lack that expertise and training, but not to the degree that should make them nervous about trying to tutor writing. Carl Smith (1993) is right when he stresses that

> Technical expertise is not necessary for adults to help young children. Parents, for example, are not expected to be professional teachers, nor to have anything more than a healthy curiosity and a willingness to work with their children in a friendly, conversational way. (14)

And Nancy Mavrogenes (1996) points out that most parents are willing to help in their children's education, but many have little idea of how to go about it. Parents need to be given some reassurance and direction that will benefit their child and not hamper the teacher. Teachers can share a simple process and several suggestions that will reassure parents, make them effective writing tutors for their children, and help teachers, too.

General Guidelines for Parents Tutoring Children

Smith tries to reassure parents by giving them the following guidelines:

- Encourage, engage in conversation, and be pleased at new knowledge and skill;
- Look for improvement in your child and in yourself as a tutor;
- Listen carefully and ask questions to clarify your child's understanding;
- Praise even small improvements because learning and improving mean making progress, not becoming perfect overnight. (14–15)

Smith believes these guidelines are within the scope of most parents' capacity and willingness and that the guidelines reassure parents that they can indeed tutor their child. He goes on to give objectives for tutoring sessions that will focus parents and show them that what they can do is important for the child's learning and success in school.

- Develop positive attitude: talk about how literacy gives us the ability to communicate and expand our lives;
- Build communication: share interesting words from reading or writing and develop comprehension by pausing every now and again to summarize our sense of how the reading and writing is developing or will develop;
- Promote critical thinking: discuss your reaction to the reading or piece of writing, raising questions about causes and consequences and talking about values you hold or you know others hold and how they are connected to the facts or events in the reading or piece of writing;
- Develop fluency: model reading and writing and discuss the reading and writing you and your child are doing. (16–17)

Strategies for Parents Tutoring Writing

In addition to Smith's guidelines, we recommend that parents choose from the processes, strategies, and goals described in Chapters 4–6. Parents tutoring writing at home can also use the following strategies.

Focus on clear/unclear. The focus in tutoring is always on the writer's meaning and the tutor's understanding. These concerns are central. Parents would be wise to be well versed in tutoring strategies that help the child see problems with clarity of meaning and understanding. Smith (1993) recommends using a string of questions that begin with "I" to show the child that the problem may be with the tutor/reader, not with the writer or the writing. Questions like "I don't see why you talk about _____ after just talking about _____" or "I am having trouble understanding _____" can take some of the sting out of criticism.

Smith also recommends that parents point out where writing is clear and easily understood. He supplies a checklist of qualities that parents can watch for and praise:

- precise vocabulary—for example, not "liked the teacher" but "admired the teacher"; not "smiled" but "smirked"
- colorful vocabulary—for example, not "laughed" but "guffawed"; not "hit the home run" but "launched a rainbow"
- orderly sequence of events or ideas that is easy to follow
- explanation of the causes/reasons for a character's actions
- description of the setting in which actions occur
- adequate detail and description to aid the reader with all of the above

Create a personal spelling dictionary.   Parents will often see spelling errors in their children's writing. Some of these errors are the result of *invented spelling*: Young or inexperienced writers will invent spellings in order to carry meaning (Bolton and Snowball 1993). Invented spellings will regularize over time because growth in spelling is directly tied to reading experience, to seeing correct spelling over and over, and to paying attention to words in all contexts, including supermarket packaging, big books for kids, newspaper headlines, birthday cards, billboards, stories, signs, and TV ads (Gentry 1996). As the child reads more, writes more, and pays attention to both, spelling becomes more regular.

With this in mind, we recommend that parent tutors encourage their children to create and keep a personal spelling dictionary (PSD), a procedure that Trevor Cairney and Lynne Munsie (1991) have shown is effective for both improving spelling and focusing tutoring sessions when spelling seems like the right topic to talk about. To create a PSD, the parent asks the child to begin a list of the words she has trouble with, including for each, one to three example sentences that show the word spelled correctly. Younger children may enjoy decorating paper pages and making a cover; all children can keep an electronic dictionary under their name in the word processing program they use most frequently. The idea of a PSD is to focus attention on spelling within the context of the child's problem words and real writing. When editing a nearly completed draft, the child can consult her paper or electronic PSD to double-check the words she has trouble with. An added benefit of using a PSD is that both child and parents will see that the child is getting better at spelling because her additions to the PSD will become less and less frequent as she grows in language experience.

Stretch beyond the tutoring session. Parents should not see tutoring as short-term but instead should attempt to use its potential for the child's entire life in school. James Alvino (1995) suggests that parents supplement school-sponsored writing, which can be infrequent or tedious, with writing done at home that arises from the interaction between parent and child during the tutoring session. He offers several activities that could be the focus of talk during tutoring:

- Real-world audiences: Letters to the editor or feature articles for school or public newspapers; letters or e-mails to people or organizations the child believes in; stories, poems, plays to send to magazines or Web-based engines geared to children's writing.

- Journals or diaries: Kept for public or personal reading, focused on an event (a vacation at the shore), a process (learning to play goal for the soccer team), a person (grandpa's wild stories), dreams (a faithful account of nightly images), or movies or TV shows (retelling, rewriting, or critiquing).

- Detailed observations: Places, things, or persons described in detail after careful observation. For example, a person might be described by what she said, the sound of her voice, the feel of her skin, and her gestures, actions, clothes, hairstyle, smell, and makeup.

A rich resource for parents who want to encourage their children to write in ways that grow out of home-tutoring interactions can be found in an appendix to Nancie Atwell's *Coming to Know: Writing to Learn in the Intermediate Grades* (1990). Atwell compiles contributions from several teachers into nearly twenty pages' worth of prompts to help young writers keep learning logs about a wide range of academic subjects and other activities (such as field trips and vacations). Parents can easily use the prompts to ask questions about animals, the community, films, fire prevention, and so on, in order to sustain their children's writing through the summer vacation months or as a supplement to school-based assignments. Paul Davis (1991) has devised a project in which parents and students write together about their childhoods.

Another way parents can be effective writing tutors is by forging strong partnerships with their children's teachers, what James Moffett (1985) calls "a new covenant between school and home." Linda Rief (1992) suggests that parents and teachers use two-way communication in the form of letters and opportunities for parents to assess writing portfolios. Three times a year, students bring their writing portfolios home, including their logs of books read, and share the contents with their parents. Each child accompanies the writing portfolio with a letter that responds to prompts like these:

- Dear Mom/Dad: This is what I've done well as a writer, reader, listener, and speaker.
- Please note that this is what I'll be attempting to do better.

Teachers can share two tips with parents who are motivated to serve as their children's writing tutors:

- Let children see you write often. You are both a model and a tutor. Occasionally read aloud what you have written and ask your children for their opinion.
- To help children appreciate the value of pieces of writing they produce at home, use their writing as gifts for relatives and family friends. (Atwell 1998)

The Pittsburgh school system's Arts PROPEL program (Daro 1993) encourages parents to become part of the reading audience of student writers by exchanging writing critiques with their children. Parents read the child's portfolio and respond to these questions:

- Which piece of writing in the folder tells you the most about your child's writing?
- What does it tell you?
- What do you see as the strengths in your child's writing?
- What do you see as needing to be addressed in your child's growth and development as a writer?
- What suggestions do you have that might aid the class's growth as writers?

After parents read and respond to the portfolios and share their comments with the children, the children react to the experience by replying to these questions:

- What do you think your parents learned about you as a writer as a result of their reading your folders and discussing them with you?
- What did you learn about yourself as a writer as a result of your discussion with your parents?
- What surprised you most about the discussion?
- What suggestions do you have that might improve your discussions with your parents about your writing?

Chapter Eight

Tutoring Different People

However varied the settings for tutoring writing may be, nothing is more varied than the people who tutor and are tutored. This chapter looks at factors that interact to form a large portion of the interpersonal and instructional context for all tutoring sessions: ability as a writer; gender; experience with mainstream English language and American culture; learning disabilities; and personality and learning styles. The chapter then discusses how these factors affect tutoring and suggests strategies for improving the effectiveness of tutoring sessions where one or more of the factors is present.

Ability Levels

When we think of a writer's ability as a factor in tutoring, it's the student, not the tutor, who most often comes to mind. Has he had much writing experience? Does he read books, newspapers, magazines? Does he enter into conversations and discussions in thoughtful and attentive ways? More writing experience, more reading, and more thoughtful talk are all characteristic of able writers.

Writing ability is a measure of the tutor, too. In the literature and discussion about tutoring writing, it is generally assumed that the tutor is an experienced and able writer, certainly more so than the person who is being tutored. Tutors are often chosen because they are recognized as good writers by their grades in English or other courses, by recommendation of teachers, or by consistently good performance with regular writing tasks. It seems reasonable that someone who is an able and experienced writer will do well at tutoring, all other things being equal.

But in real-world situations, the distance between the tutor's ability and the writer's ability can narrow. For example, the chemistry teacher, who wants tutors who have completed her course, finds that the only students available to tutor are those who don't go on to the next course. She must pick from this pool even if some were only average in their writing of chemistry assignments. Or the writing center director puts out a call for tutors and finds that only some of those who apply have both the writing ability and personality he had hoped for, so center staff is then a mix of ability and personality.

We think it's fine for the ability levels of tutor and writer to be closer than it's normally assumed they'll be. After all, the tutor/writer relationship should be closer than the expert/novice or editor/rookie relationship. Tutors need to be decent at writing, care about doing it well, and care about helping others. Peer response groups work well even when writers are of similar ability because everyone can learn something from the different strengths and perspectives of others, and typically everyone wants to be helpful to group members. Ability is enhanced by a commitment to tutoring and by caring for the other, be she writer or tutor.

Tutors should be aware of the effects the writer's ability can have on their tutoring practice and process. Writers make things happen to themselves, both positive and negative, in the conversational environment of a tutorial. Sarah Freedman and Melanie Sperling (1985) were among the first researchers to look at the effect of ability on tutor/writer interaction, in this case in writing conferences between a college classroom teacher and students. They found that high ability writers are tutor/teacher smart. They make tutor-pleasing statements ("I really admire people who can write well") that not only encourage the tutor to make positive inferences about them, but that also build closer rapport. High ability writers are also good at eliciting praise from tutors by using self-deprecating statements ("I still don't think I'm that good a writer"). G. G. Patthey-Chavez and Dana Ferris (1997) found that high ability writers are more assertive than weaker writers in expressing their opinions about writing and issues, are better at eliciting teacher feedback about what is important to them, and are better at getting longer conferences—as much as 50 percent longer than weaker writers' conferences. Freedman and Sperling also found that low ability writers make statements that are potentially tutor-alienating ("I like working better than going to school") and often give inappropriate back-channel cues, showing both the desire to join in the tutoring conversation and a lack of know-how. When weaker writers initiate a conversation topic, they focus on HOCs and LOCs without prioritizing, as if they have trouble distinguishing what is important. The emerging portrait of ability's effect on tutoring puts high ability writers in more control of the tutorial.

Freedman and Sperling found that tutors working with strong writers make discourse-level topics as the focus of talk, while tutors working with weaker writers deal with discourse and correctness issues equally, perhaps responding to the student's lack of a priority of concerns. This is important: Freedman and Sperling go on to identify discourse-level focus as being characteristic of the revision that is most improved after a tutoring session. They also report that tutors speak to high ability writers in a more academic register, reserving a more colloquial tone for weaker writers. Tutors also tend to be more enthusiastic when they invite stronger writers to return for future tutoring. Patthey-Chavez and Ferris report that tutors are less directive and more collaborative with strong writers, sharing time and agenda issues. It would seem, then, that the presence of a strong writer loads the dice in favor of a strong tutoring session.

The best way to work with writers of varying ability is to treat them all as if they are high ability writers. We suggest the following strategies:

- Focus on discourse-level topics as a priority for all writers, making surface correctness a second-tier priority; perhaps even teaching the concept of a priority of concerns to weaker writers so that they begin to realize that development is in most cases more important than a correctness issue such as spelling.
- Use an appropriate register for speaking, monitoring yourself to ensure that you give all students experience with an academic register.
- Enthusiastically invite all to return with future drafts and revisions, even scheduling appointments for weaker writers on the spot.
- Ignore antiwriting or antischool comments, whoever makes them.
- Talk around inappropriate back-channel cues.
- Most important, realize that what happens during a conference is the product of the two people who are interacting, a synthesis of their speech and behaviors, as well as of the piece of writing itself.

Even with these guidelines, tutors express some uneasiness when they are asked to tutor a writer they perceived as a better writer than themselves. To help alleviate their concerns, we show them Winston Weathers' (1980) ideas about *Grammar B*, which he claims exists alongside traditional grammar, *Grammar A*, in the work of writers as diverse as Tom Wolfe, Will and Ariel Durant, Gertrude Stein, Norman Mailer, D. H. Lawrence, Virginia Woolf, E. M. Forster, Emily Dickinson, and others. The best writers learn Grammar B as they try to expand upon the limitations of Grammar A. We use Grammar B in the same way with tutors, helping better writers use it to expand what they can do. Weathers describes Grammar B as an alternate style, one that's not taught in school, that is characterized by features like those listed below. We show these features to our tutors. We also give tutors copies of Tom Romano's (1988) description of Grammar B in the writing of elementary and secondary students, and encourage them to read *Elements of Alternate Style*, a 1997 collection of essays on writing and revision, edited by Wendy Bishop, that discusses Grammar B and alternate style issues in college composition theory and pedagogy.

Weathers' Grammar B Features

Sentence fragment. A word. Or a short phrase. Used for emphasis, variety, or sound. Allowed for with the best writers but typically marked wrong for weaker ones.

Labyrinthine sentence. The labyrinthine sentence is a long complex sentence, full of convolutions, digressions, appositives, embeddings, dashes, and parentheses, creating a flow, like a river washing downstream over rocks, sandbars, and fallen trees (except, of course, in winter), or creating a run, like a marathon runner puffing, puffing, puffing uphill, wiping sweat, the by-product of the energy burnt to push forward, twenty-six miles of exertion, all with the love of the motion and anticipation of the end—an end that feels as if it is off in the distance for both runner and reader of the sentence. We have tutors look at many models of the labyrinthine sentence, among them the 119-word opening sentence to Thomas Pynchon's *Mason and Dixon* (1997) and some of the complicated, graceful, and lengthy lines in John Lahr's *New Yorker* theater reviews.

Crots. *Crots* are like stanzas in poetry. They are "chunks" or "blocks" of sentences with little connection to what came before or after. They lack transitions on either end and stand as autonomous devices, creating the effect of jumping from one issue to another, much like modern conversation, TV news, and life experience in general. Crots are connected in whatever way by the readers, uniquely, while the readers are simultaneously aware of each crot's separateness.

Double voice. Chapter 6 describes methods for clarifying and creating voice. In Grammar B, *voice* becomes *voices*. The writer adopts multiple voices, positions, or perspectives instead of one. When the writer sees two or more sides of an issue as valid and reasonable, she can present them; when she feels two or more emotions arise in a situation, she can portray them. Multiple voices are presented simultaneously, with formatting and typographic devices such as columns, indentation, and italics used to distinguish between voices while suggesting the simultaneity of the perspectives or emotions. Pulitzer Prize–winning columnist Maureen Dowd (1999) provides a model of the double voice, reproducing the letter that Charlton Heston wrote to National Rifle Association members in the aftermath of the tragic school shooting in Littleton, Colorado. Dowd periodically interrupts the letter's text with her own interpretations, set in italics, of what she imagines Heston's *real* thoughts to be.

Collage/montage. In collage/montage, diverse elements of both Grammar B and traditional style are patched together to create the piece of writing, with the effect of wholeness achieved from the synthesis of diverse parts.

Other Grammar B Features

Tom Romano (1995) suggests that tutors can help motivate talented writers by encouraging them to take risks by experimenting with other Grammar B language and style features. He recommends the following:

Repetition. Tutors can be shown how repetition is a staple of effective writing. Writers repeat sounds, words, ideas, and parallel patterns of phrases and sentences to achieve certain effects. Tutors can look to Frank McCourt's description of how the masters at Leamy's National School found reasons to strike students (*Angela's Ashes,* 1996) or Allen Ginsberg's use of the phrase "Is About" in his 1996 poem of that name for models of skillful repetition.

Lists. By presenting information in list form, a writer can quickly swamp the reader with details and impressions. The items in a list usually add up to make a single statement or suggest a theme. For example, when William Least Heat-Moon interrupts his conventionally presented text in *Blue Highways* (1991) to break out his observations about the desert in the American Southwest into a thirty-item list, he dramatically demonstrates that the common notion of the desert being devoid of life and activity is a myth.

Orthographic variation. Tutors see how writers yield exciting, inventive results by using calculated misspelling or controlled respelling and by altering the appearance of the words on a page (by changing case, typefaces, and type size). Tom Wolfe, John Dos Passos, and Douglas Copeland are some of the authors whose works we share to demonstrate the power of orthographic variation. Better, we share examples of how other tutors have successfully ventured into this area of style. Here's how one of our peer tutors, Jeff, leads off a piece about his experiences running practices as a basketball coach for an eighth-grade girl's team (after this lead, the rest of the piece was written in traditional prose):

> Stoplineitup. Two lines. Get those balls over your head. Fasternow. Runitlikeyoumeanit. Meanitlikeyoumeanit. Let'sgo. Let'sgo. Letsgooo. Coomeon. Twomore. FasterNicole.
> 　Twomoreifwedon'tpickitup. LookatOlivia. Great job kid. G r e a t j o b k i d. Sprintupheadupsprintupheadup-sprintupheadupheadupheadup ComeonStephaneeeeeee. Finishstrong. Pushithard. Good job. Balls on the rack please.

One final resource for demonstrating unorthodox writing styles is *Adios, Strunk and White* (Hoffman and Hoffman 1997). This book not only suggests inventive "counterculture" style techniques to which the authors give labels like "time warping" and "recyclables," but also provides abundant examples.

Gender Differences

In the last twenty-plus years, many researchers and scholars have examined the intersection of gender with both oral and written communication. Not surprisingly, they have found that gender is a powerful factor in communicative interactions. The work of Deborah Tannen (1990), Julia Wood (1994), and Barbara Eakins and Gene Eakins (1978) describes traits of male and female communicators. According to this body of research, males are generally frank, straightforward, analytic, objective, assertive, and speakers. Females tend to be cooperative, deferent, sensitive, caring, supportive, and listeners. These gender roles express themselves in the tutoring situation, whether we look at tutor or writer.

This has been documented in classroom peer response groups by Elizabeth Sommers (1992) and in writing center tutorials by Joyce Kinkead (1985), Jean Kiedaisch and Sue Dinitz (1991), and Kathleen Hunzer (1994). Sommers, studying peer response groups in a college composition class, found that two types of groups developed: *communal*, in which males and females were talkative, supportive, and attentive and took risks because they felt they had authority over their own learning, and *compliant*, in which males were more assertive and talkative while females were reticent and seemed lacking in authority. Sommers argues that individuals in groups need to be willing to go beyond prescribed gender roles to take on roles that facilitate the group functioning. She concludes that one of the skills of good teaching is the ability to create a classroom community that allows people to enact these facilitating roles, when necessary by adding special support to help women students move from the "good girl" reticence of the compliant group to the riskier talkativeness of the communal group.

Kinkead found the same gender stereotypes in writing center tutorials. Female tutors were often effective questioners, drawing writers into the session's process and agenda, and they consistently focused on discourse-level HOCs. Male tutors were often directive and prescriptive, especially about traditional teacherly things like paragraphing and punctuation. Kiedaisch and Dinitz found a gender difference in the effectiveness ratings of tutoring sessions, with females being ranked the highest overall and the most effective pairing of tutor/writer being female/female. Hunzer detailed the reasons behind the effectiveness of the female/female pairing, finding that female writers preferred the sociability, solicitude, and self-expressive tendencies of female tutors. She also found that male writers preferred the directiveness, assertiveness, and analytical style of male tutors.

Because both male and female tutors communicated along expected stereotypical lines, these studies suggest that the gender roles imposed by culture supercede any training tutors might receive. The training we get from culture, which is far more expansive and lasts far longer than any training in tutoring could, dominates communication situations. Although more tutor training might help reduce the negative effect of cultural stereotyping about gender—especially training in sensitivity to the full spectrum of possible tutorial roles—the power of gender roles can actually be put to use in tutoring situations by following these recommendations:

- Use the inherent power of gender communication stereotypes by connecting writers to male tutors when analysis, directiveness, or assertiveness seem to be what the writer's developing skills call for, and to female tutors when supportive, caring, and cooperative interactions seem most productive. To do this, someone would have to decide which qualities a writer most needed in a tutor. This could be done by having a tutor, at the end of a session, recommend a gender-specific tutor assignment for the next session, or by having a senior tutor do an initial screening.

- Resist gender communication stereotype—they are nothing more than the expression of sexism in our culture. Train tutors to reach beyond these stereotypes and develop a balanced "whole human" approach to that emphasizes appropriate strategies and behaviors for each writer at each session, with the tutor being directive or supportive, analytic or caring, as the tutoring process demands.

• In writing centers and offices where groups of tutors are available, try to have both genders represented at all times so that writers can self-select what they feel they need. In classrooms where the teacher has no alternative, she can be aware of the demonstrated power of gender in tutoring and strive for a "whole human" stance.

Multicultural and ESL Writers and Tutors

In the last thirty years, classrooms and workplaces have become more ethnically, racially, and culturally diverse. We can expect that diversity to grow if government projections are accurate. Immigration, the internationalization of corporations, international students, and a larger portion of current Americans moving through the educational system all point to a very different experience in school and college classrooms, writing centers, and on the job. Those who would tutor writers in any of these venues would be wise to change the way they understand tutoring, if their understanding is grounded in a monocultural and English-only perspective.

Writers now arrive at class with experiences that are far different than the ones writers had in the monolinguistic past. Some universities report that students who are enrolled in English as a second language (ESL) programs represent more than twenty-five languages. A twelfth-grade teacher from Sacramento, California, told us that twenty-two different language groups were represented in his five sections of senior English. One of our neighbors, an engineer with a major multinational corporation, was the only Caucasian English speaker on his ten-person project team.

We believe that writers and tutors from different cultures and with different home languages can work together. Diversity within classes can lead to a blossoming of human understanding across cultural and linguistic boundaries, and to a refinement and enrichment of tutoring itself as one-to-one instruction creates a space for connection across boundaries. Tutoring can allow students who feel marginalized by their culture or language, or who feel disconnected from American academic culture, to develop their own academic voices and established their place in current campus life.

Because ESL writers and tutors have backgrounds different from those of the monolinguistic groups in which tutoring procedures were developed, ESL writers will require a perhaps substantial modification of those procedures. Lynn Goldstein and Susan Conrad (1990) demonstrated that the conference procedures American teachers use with ESL students, especially non-Western students, are quite different from the ones they use with college students whose native language is English. Such differences can be good when they address the specific needs of ESL writers.

Judith Powers (1993) reports that the tutoring at her writing center changed dramatically with a threefold increase in ESL writers. She characterized the change as calling into question one of the central tenets of conferencing: that the tutor should proceed nondirectively, without prescribing, drawing the writer into seeing and taking action on problems in process and product. Powers realized that tutors had to intervene more directly with ESL writers than with native English speakers. John Reid (1994) shows that it is possible to intervene in the writing process of ESL writers without appropriating their texts and voices, which would violate a central tenet of tutoring.

When a native English speaker asks for direct intervention ("Could you check it to see if it's right?"), we may think the writer lacks confidence because he has little experience with writing or because of the grammar/phonics/correctness pedagogy followed in too many American schools. Or we may think that the writer is looking for the easy way out on a class assignment. Powers reminds us that when ESL writers ask for direct intervention, they are usually motivated by a lack of linguistic, rhetorical, and academic knowledge. Tutors working with ESL writers must be ready to become more like traditional teachers and less like helpful collaborators. As Powers says, teaching ESL writers may involve, especially initially, "teaching them directly what their writing should look like . . . informing them of what their audiences will expect" (34). Johns (1995) believes that the pedagogy of the helpful collaborator, no matter how well intentioned, is "cruelly unfair" to ESL writers because it does not give them the background knowledge that their tutors and native speakers generally have, leaving them at a disadvantage when approaching writing tasks in other classes or on the job.

With this in mind, let us make recommendations for recruiting and training multicultural tutors and for working with ESL writers, all of whom are part of the multicultural and ESL diversity of our schools and workplaces.

Recruiting and Training Multicultural Tutors

Gail Okawa et al. (1991) point to several helpful tactics for recruiting and training multicultural writing center tutors:

- Recruit tutors to mirror the cultural, gender, class, and linguistic diversity of the writers who visit the center. Finding willing tutors with these characteristics can be difficult. Okawa et al. suggest finding tutors by establishing close ties with administrative divisions and programs that support international students or special-admission native English speakers, or by considering regular visitors to the writing center as potential tutors. Roger Hooper (1993) reports success in using students in advanced ESL classes as tutors for lower level independent study students.

- Once a multicultural staff of tutors is established, use training that does the following:

> Considers that both tutor and writer come to a tutoring session with expectations and behaviors that are culturally derived, even native speakers from dominant groups.

> Uses active "self-discovering" in which tutors engage in critical reflection about their own and their writers' values and assumptions about literacy and language, interaction with others, and the means and ends of schooling.

> Explores how the institution itself is shot through with hierarchies that reduce the chances for and effectiveness of more democratic instructional strategies like tutoring and writing centers.

Working with ESL Writers

Once tutors are recruited and receive general training, they need to expand their repertoires to include strategies that will allow them to deal with the characteristics of ESL writing and writers. Muriel Harris and Tony Silva (1993) supply a number of these:

- Plunging in: ESL writing often seems plagued by miscues at all levels. Tutors need to be reminded to maintain a hierarchy of concerns, HOCs before LOCs; focus on one or just a few problems at a time; and explain to writers that miscues are a natural part of learning and using language, even for native speakers.

- Contrastive rhetorics: Tutors need to both know and explain to writers that all cultures produce rhetorical preferences, all of which are equally good and potent, and that the set of American academic English rhetorical preferences is just one among them.

- Linguistic transfer: The issue of first language (L1) features transferring to second language (L2) writing has a contentious history in ESL research. L1 transfer may happen sometimes, causing problems in L2. But many more reasons (such as good or poor L1 or L2 instruction, experience writing in L1 and L2) help to explain ESL writing problems. Tutors should not dismiss an ESL writing problem as an example of L1 transference without knowing about the writer's previous instruction (Did it cover grammar/correctness vs. meaning/use?) and experience (Was it mostly oral and reading, with little writing?).

▪ Behavior patterns: Culturally derived behavioral differences can inhibit interaction. One culture might encourage eye contact while another discourages it; one might value punctuality while another doesn't; one might favor tight physical proximity while another prefers loose proximity. It's important to be aware of these and similar concerns when doing multicultural tutoring.

▪ Teaching patterns: Many cultures have a very different view of teaching—of teacher, student, and classroom—than the one that's inherent in tutoring, the view that tutoring is conversational, one-to-one, in-process pedagogy. Many ESL students have a much more authoritarian view of teachers. They don't question teachers and don't expect to be questioned by them, as usually happens in a tutoring session; instead, they expect to give answers as direct statements.

▪ Proficiency vs. process: All writers must have a reasonable amount of proficiency in English before they can deal with the writing process. Tutors need to be ready to give basic English instruction or to refer writers to ESL specialists who can get them over that initial hurdle.

▪ More writing time: Tutors can help ESL writers do more initial generating and planning, help them prioritize HOCs and LOCs, and give them more rereading and reflection time to allow for the slower writing and reading pace of many ESL writers.

▪ Grammar and error: Grammatical problems will occur less frequently as the writer acquires more experience in English. When ESL writers seek editing-only conferences, question why LOCs should be dealt with before HOCs, or demand to know rules of correctness, the tutor can describe the priority of concerns in tutoring and the hierarchy of importance in language and writing, reminding the students that they can't expect their writing to be as error-free as that of people who have used English all their lives. To show that the writer's concerns are part of the negotiated agenda of a tutoring session, tutors should address such concerns in the session they come up in.

Terese Thonus (1993) supplies several valuable issues and strategies for working with ESL writers:

- World Englishes: English is now spoken by over a billion people, most of whom are not native speakers. Anyone who teaches English in a multicultural setting should be aware that "English" is not one language, but that it exists in many varieties across cultures.

- World ESL students: ESL students study English for a variety of reasons and with varied commitment and results. They are no different from native American students of English, who also have diverse motivations. Tutors should avoid developing a single "cookie-cutter" strategy that they use with all ESL students.

- Use the native language: Although conventional wisdom was to discourage ESL students from using their native languages, recent research encourages native language usage, keeping the writer focused on HOCs and the writing's developing meaning.

- Be positive: Tutors should create rapport by discussing a particular feature of the ESL writer's work early on in the tutoring process. The elaborate and decorative style of some Spanish-speaking writers can be complimented even when they are learning the concise "get to the point" style of English. The indirectness used by some Asian writers can be deemed appropriate to American culture even if the tutor feels it isn't appropriate to American academic writing.

Learning Disabled Writers

Tutors at work, at home, and in school may assist writers who are learning disabled. Learning disabled writers often come to tutoring with a long history of frustration at low grades and low self-esteem. Tutors should be aware that learning disabled writers do not produce illegible, error-filled pieces out of laziness or carelessness. They may write very little and mask writing flaws in illegibility. Because they are retreating from painful past experiences with writing, their behaviors might at first range from quiet noncompliance to outright aggression.

Perhaps the most important step tutors can take when meeting with learning disabled writers is to set up a risk-free environment that lets writers relax and rethink their ill will toward writing. Tutors can use the following strategies to boost the self-image of learning disabled writers and to ease them into more productive encounters with the act of writing:

- If writers have visual processing disorders, they have trouble keeping up and copying notes from the chalkboard. Tutors can recommend that these writers use a tape recorder in class and during tutorial session to assist them with note-taking. In institutions where specials services are available to learning disabled students, a student might be assigned a note taker.

- Tutors can remind learning disabled writers that tape-recorded textbooks are available from the organization Recordings for the Blind and Dyslexic.

- If writers have short-term memory problems, they may recall and write steps in the wrong order. If they have long-term memory problems, they may forget key concepts. A writing tutor may need to constantly review the steps and concepts that come up in a tutorial conversation. The tutor should explain things slowly and emphasize major points.

- There is a fair amount of evidence that using spelling-checker software benefits learning disabled writers. Thus, tutor and writer could arrange to use a computer during tutoring sessions.

- Some learning disabled writers may compose productively by dictating to the tutor, who transcribes the writer's piece.

- Tutors should be prepared to budget more time for tutorial sessions with learning disabled writers.

Personalities and Learning Styles

An indispensable resource for writing tutors is the Myers-Briggs Type Indicator (MBTI), a validated self-reporting instrument whose internal and test/retest consistency has proven to be respectable (Myers and McCaulley 1985). The MBTI model identifies four different preferences individuals use to conduct their daily lives. These preferences seem to have specific implications for revealing writers' composing processes, as well as for guiding tutoring strategies.

According to the theory, each of us favors one of two orientations—extroversion or introversion; one of two ways of taking in information—sensing or intuiting; one of two ways of making decisions—thinking or feeling; and one of two ways of approaching the outer world—judging or perceiving. Research about the MBTI (DiTiberio and Jensen 1994; Cramer and Reigstad 1994) indicates that extroverts work best when allowed to talk out loud about their writing. They also benefit from strategies like free writing and may not revise unless they get feedback. Introverts, on the other hand, work best when they think before they write. They benefit from systematic ways to explore a writing project. Sensing types like it when discussions begin with concrete facts and examples. Intuitive types prefer conversations that begin with theories and inferences, and often write first drafts that are overgeneralized and lack solid examples. Judging types of writers enjoy structure, and hold to a work schedule. Perceiving types find it hard to focus, may write at the last minute, and often produce rambling, expansive pieces.

Thomas Thompson (1994) believes that writing tutors can gain by becoming more sensitive to how their own tutoring styles clash or mesh with writers' preferred learning styles. For example, thinking types of tutors seem to prefer to hold businesslike conferences, whereas feeling types prefer to begin sessions with small talk.

Even if tutors don't have writers' MBTI preferences at hand, merely knowing that individual differences exist can help them communicate that the writer's preferences are writing strengths. Tutors can gently nudge writers toward using their less dominant preferences in ways that will broaden their problem-solving repertoire. For example, an extrovert who always begins writing without written brainstorming might be encouraged to give it a try.

Another way for tutors to consider individual learning styles is through the lens of Howard Gardner's (1985) theory of multiple intelligences. Gardner says that humans display intelligence of at least seven types: linguistic; logical-mathematical; spatial; bodily-kinesthetic; musical; interpersonal; and intrapersonal. Tutors who know about this theory might help the whole writer by allowing opportunities for various types of intelligence to be manifested in writing. For example, they might tap the strengths of a bodily-kinesthetic writer by doing breathing exercises in a tutoring session.

Writers displaying logical-mathematical intelligence might be shown the logic of several prewriting heuristics. Tutors can help spatially oriented writers by pointing out how formatting writing (with typefaces, spacing, and so on) contributes to its effectiveness. Tutors may even find the right background music to inspire writers who display musical intelligence.

Chapter Nine

Lessons from the Masters

In this chapter we'll acquaint you with some of the best-and-brightest figures in the field of tutoring writers. Their contributions to the theory and practice of writing instruction are groundbreaking, practical, and enduring.

Donald M. Murray

> I would try to have the students speak first. In the beginning, students are not used to me. I ask them questions such as "How's it going?" and "What do you think of the piece?" These rather open-ended questions force them to make a commitment before I do. As my students become experienced with me, they will just come in and start talking to me because they know that it is their job to talk. So, the dynamics of conferencing are for me to listen and to get them to say whatever is helpful. I think it's better for the student to discover it for themselves and better for me to evaluate what the student is saying. (1979a)

Donald Murray has been called the "apostle of conferencing" (McCleary 1988). In his many years as professor of English at the University of New Hampshire, where he is now professor emeritus, Murray had a huge impact on how writing was taught there and at other universities around the country. His teaching method of choice was tutoring. In "The Listening Eye: Reflections on the Writing Conference" (1979b), Murray describes conducting seventy-five writing tutorials a week, thirty weeks a year. He customarily conducted one-to-one meetings on campus and tried to make the atmosphere conducive to learning:

> In my office in the university I try to create an environment where I am comfortable and relaxed and informal. I've dragged in a rug on the floor to cut down the resonance. There is a big clock that I can see—where the students can't—so I can keep some idea of what's going on. (14)

Some terms central to understanding Murray's tutoring philosophy are *listening*, *discovery*, and the writer's *other self*. Although Murray promotes listening as a vital function of a writing tutor, he says that tutors need to nurture listening as a natural function in writers themselves:

> The act of writing might be described as a conversation between two workmen muttering to each other. The self speaks, the other self listens and responds. (1982b, 145)

Murray urges tutors to model an ideal other self by asking questions that lead writers to discover that the big matters of content, meaning, and focus need to be confronted first:

> What's the single most important thing you have to say?
>
> What questions is the reader going to ask you and when are they going to be asked?
>
> Where do you hear the voice come through strongest?

In Murray's view, it is the tutor's duty to help the writer find the other self by asking questions that the writer thinks have no answers—but that the writer in fact knows the answers to:

> Why did you use such a strong word here?
>
> How did you cut this description and make it clearer?
>
> Why did you add so many specifics on page 39?
>
> I think this ending works, but what did you see that made you realize that old beginning was the new ending?

Murray invents several metaphors to describe his preferred stance for a writing tutor. One metaphor depicts an inspirational jogging partner:

> I think students need the experience of writing and they need to have somebody running along beside them while they have this experience of writing. (1979a, 2)

Another Murray metaphor for tutoring writers is as voice coach:

> If I had to have a term [for writing tutor], I think 'coach' is a much better one in terms of voice coach, where the person sings or says a

part and the coach tries to help them bring the part out or bring the song out. (1979a, 4)

By assuming these facilitative roles, writing tutors take a nondirective approach that draws out writers and enables them to explore their strengths and weaknesses.

Listening is perhaps the tutor's most critical act in a Murray-style conference, especially at the beginning of a session. Murray isn't above throwing the ball into the writer's conversational court from the outset of a conference by posing the most general and open of questions, as he did with Laura:

Murray: So?

Laura: Umm (laughter) Well, I've started working on my other one, my other article. And what I did for starters was to talk to my nutrition teacher and he suggested that if I was to do this that I should do it from the viewpoint of strictly health foods.

Murray: Yeah.

Laura: And not do, and deal mostly with the natural foods store and that sort of thing. (Reigstad 1980)

Even though he once listed a set of the right questions to ask at the start of a writing tutorial, Murray (1979b) believes that ideally writers will eventually learn to ask these questions of themselves before they even show up for tutoring:

What did you learn from this piece of writing?

What do you intend to do in the next draft?

What surprised you in the draft?

Where is the piece of writing taking you?

What do you like best in the piece of writing?

What questions do you have of me?

Murray doesn't simply sit back and listen: He usually reaches a stage in the tutor-writer interaction where he actively engages in exploratory, off-the-paper talk in order to help the writer generate information and ideas for the paper, or to act himself as a general resource. With Laura, who is still in the fact-finding stage of writing about health food, Murray suggests, well into their conference, looking into health food markets. Minutes later he brings up a personal anecdote related to Laura's topic:

Murray: Yeah, yeah, good. Where are the places that you plan to go?

Laura: Well, he told me to just basically do my own investigating, to look in as many health food stores as I can.

Murray: Yeah. Are you going to Boston for some? I wouldn't necessarily, but if you are, Erewhon is the biggest company in the area. There's one on Milbury Street and there's one in Cambridge.

Laura: Um-hmm.

Murray: And I wouldn't necessarily go to them, because I think there's enough nuts around here that you could . . . (laughter) with Portsmouth and New Market and Exeter, and you know, gee whiz.

Laura: Uh-huh. . . .

Murray: A lot of people who are health nuts here get their stuff imported from there here in town. We had dinner at a friend's house where everything was pure.

Laura: Um-hmm.

Murray: That was the big point. They've got disgusting, funny-looking food. It tasted okay, some of it wasn't that great. But, by God, it was pure!

By the end of the one-to-one meeting, Murray steers the writer toward possibly including the high price of health food products as a controlling idea in her paper:

Murray: I think some limiting of it . . . I usually like the idea of focus, but I think you might come back from the health food stores . . . I guess I'm not as worried about the consumer who bothers to go to a specialty store like Common Market. I guess I'm a little more consumer concerned about the rip-offs of the . . .

Laura: The price, yeah.

Murray: —the candy bars in other places and things that are bought in Shop 'N Save.

Laura: I think that's going to be a big thing in it.

Laura, and most likely other writers tutored by Murray, recognized his artful switching of roles, from passive listener to active participant, in the structure of a given conference. Tom Reigstad (1979) wrote this:

> Most of my conferences with Don Murray began with his question, "Well, how did you feel about this paper?" His technique was not to tell me the good and poor aspects of my writing, but to manipulate my thinking in such a way that I could find and separate these aspects for myself. (1)

Roger H. Garrison

> You're going to have to read very fast and you're going to do no rambling role during conferences. This is business. So you read the draft in front of you, you comment to the student, and you keep a priority checklist in your mind. (1979a)

Roger Garrison did for a generation of two-year college writing teachers/tutors what Murray did at the four-year college level. Working out of his home base at Westbrook College in Portland, Maine, Garrison espoused a tutoring-only methodology of writing instruction and conducted training workshops at community colleges from coast to coast. In one case, after forty-six English teachers in the Los Angeles Community College District attended one of his tutoring seminars, four of the campuses taught writing exclusively by tutoring. The formal experiment resulted in the "Garrison approach" (that is, tutoring only) leading to "greater gains in writing ability" than those made in non-Garrison writing classes (Simmons 1979).

Garrison was known for running brief, efficient four-to-five-minute writing tutorials (the "quick conference approach"). His modus operandi was to follow a sequence of priorities. Garrison's writing tutor is a good listener, a fast reader, a skilled diagnostician, and an editor-on-the-spot. The tutor's ability to immediately zero in on the most significant problem area evolves over time:

> By this time I've literally had thousands of conferences and it becomes instinctive to ask the appropriate questions, to scan a student draft and be able to spot the trouble or the possibility for improvement. (1979a)

New writing tutors can rely on Garrison's order of priorities to guide their decision making. Garrison recommends that the tutor first read the draft quickly and look for a strength, any strength. The tutor then asks questions such as: "What are you trying to tell me here?" and "How does this statement follow the one before?" and "I like this short example—what more do you want to say about it?" Finally, the tutor makes two or three specific suggestions about what to do next, turns the work back to the writer, and closes the session (1981b).

Garrison's six essential priorities that a tutor must tend to in the following order are:

1. idea or subject
2. content
3. point of view
4. organization

5. sentences

6. diction

He describes these priorities in two publications for tutors (1974; 1981b) and in the 1985 writing textbook that he wrote in three drafts over thirty-five days by working eight to ten hours a day (1981a). Garrison believed these steps a writer needs to master are the same as the priorities a writing tutor should follow in a quick conference. In order to make optimum use of time in a limited tutorial session, Garrison's tutor works at writing problems systematically:

> If a student's paper is too general and poorly organized, if it jumps from one point of view to another, and if it is marred with bad grammar and many misspellings, the student's first job is to attack the spongy generalizing. Until he licks that problem, he shouldn't even be asked to handle the others—and you shouldn't waste time or energy even identifying them. (1974)

Garrison's intense, fast-paced one-to-one meetings followed not only his priorities list but a general tutoring motto as well: "One problem at a time, and the most important problem first" (1974). This motto enabled him to read the writer's paper, diagnose a problem, suggest a solution or two, and end the session. Garrison preferred the metaphor of "apprentices" for the writers he tutored, a stance he felt helped narrow the "psychic Grand Canyon" that can exist between inexperienced writers and veteran teachers/tutors, and he stressed the importance of establishing an "atmosphere of nonpunitive discussion" in tutoring sessions (1979a).

One of Garrison's college freshmen, Andrea, brought this draft with her to a tutoring session:

The April Amble Road Race

> The Westbrook College students in Recreational Leadership are holding the 3rd anual April Amble Road race. The Race will be held april 28, 1979. It will begin at 12:00 noon. Entries should be here by 11:30. The registration fee is $3.00. There will be refreshments for the people who watch. The race course is 5 miles long. It will start & finish at Westbrook College. There will be awards for the winners in each division. The students are expecting 300 entries You could be one of them. There is no age limit. so everyone is welcome. See you there!

In the ensuing tutorial conversation, notice how Garrison defers commenting on the spelling, capitalization and run-on miscues (saving them for a subsequent session), instead focusing first on what he identifies as a high priority shortcoming—the paper's purpose and audience:

Andrea: You said do something on public relations.

Garrison: Oh, yes.

Andrea: And I wrote it kind of like a newspaper. Is that, I didn't know if that's what you wanted or not.

Garrison: That's fine. Well, I think I suggested that to you.

Andrea: Yeah, you said something about a newspaper, but I didn't know if that's . . .

Garrison: Well, let's see how you've done this. [Garrison reads silently] Ah, this is for runners and joggers, isn't it?

Andrea: Um-hmm.

Garrison: Okay, I think I'd put that in the lead sentence if I were you. Because the title of the event is not entirely clear to the reader who knows nothing about the background of what you say, so when you say is "for runners and joggers," you're adding this information that the reader needs.

Andrea: Um-hmm.

Garrison: Now, here, take these two sentences and show me how you can save a couple of words here.

Andrea: "The race will . . . "

Garrison: Ah, the sentences themselves are perfectly all right. But I want you to see where you can save a couple of words.

Andrea: Okay, "After that later it will begin?"

Garrison: No. You can save two. See? [Garrison adds "-ing" to paper] "Beginning at."

Andrea: Okay.

Garrison: You can make one sentence out of it instead of two. Okay?

Andrea: Okay. Um-hmm. I don't know if this should be, is that what they would call them, "entries?" The people, I couldn't think of.

Garrison: Yes. Actually, what I would do is, the entry blank, or something, has to be filled in?

Andrea: Yes.

Garrison: Well, then I would say, "entry blanks." Okay?

Andrea: Well, this is the people who are already entered.

Garrison: Oh. Oh, no wonder you had a question about that! (Laughter.) No, then I would try something like this: "Those entered in the race should be . . . " Now where is, here, remember you're a reader here at the college, "each division . . . " What are the divisions? You're not sure?

Andrea: There's different ones, there's different age . . .

Garrison: Age groups?

Andrea: Yeah.

Garrison: Well, I think you can solve that either by first finding out what the divisions are . . .

Andrea: They are just different age groups. Would I have to mention age group divisions?

Garrison: Oh, all right. Then, I would help the reader "age group divisions." Fine. See, because then that adjective qualifies that enough for a reader who doesn't know anything about it. To know this group by ages instead of whether you've got one-legged races, two-legged . . . (Laughter.)

Andrea: Okay.

Garrison: [Pointing at closing phrase, "See you there!"] You never put that kind of thing in a piece like this. Okay?

Andrea: Yeah, I wasn't sure if I should or not.

Garrison: Now I want you to take it back and to tighten it up just a little bit more. If you can get any more significant information, particularly toward the beginning. For instance, the building at which they're going to meet would be useful. What building? And, or where on the campus? Are they going to meet in the cemetery where they're going to run, or what? I'm serious. The purpose of a news piece like this is to transmit information in the most economical fashion that you can. So you compress as much as you can into a short piece for newspaper use. Okay? This would be about two inches long.

Andrea: Um-hmm.

Garrison: And don't recopy it. I want to see what you're doing in between the lines.

Andrea: All right.

Garrison: Okay.

This session took just three minutes and thirty seconds.

Garrison perfected the quick, efficient, helpful writing tutorial that's businesslike yet cordial. And although the basic framework, controlled by its recipe of priorities, seems to lock a tutor into a rigid, step-by-step method, Garrison once implored one of us to instead view his approach as actually allowing flexibility for tutors: "For God's sake, don't use my model as *the* formula for tutorial instruction" (1981a).

Donald H. Graves

Action in conferences is redefined as intelligent reaction. (1983, 127)

Donald Graves, professor emeritus at the University of New Hampshire, has spent much of his career studying the writing process of children. From that unique vantage point, he has developed a theory of education in which tutoring plays a vital role. If listening is central to Donald Murray's philosophy of tutoring, it absolutely dominates Graves', who feels that in a typical tutorial episode with young writers, the tutor should speak just 20 percent of the time, the writer 80 percent. He even recommends that writing tutors make an effort to wait patiently for fifteen to twenty seconds if necessary after posing a question, to give the writer a chance to respond.

Graves offers valuable counsel for writing tutors of all stripes: teachers, parents, and peers. He makes important distinctions between types of writing tutorials and stages within a tutorial. His tutoring theory has evolved over the years, too. Overall, Graves urges tutors to probe writers for a sense of a three-dimensional history of the paper under discussion. Three basic questions are helpful for eliciting information from the writer about the past, present, and future of a paper:

Where did the paper come from?

Where is the piece now?

Where will the piece be going?

As tutors enable writers to explain what they are doing, Graves says tutors should always look for a "teachable moment" and pause for a quick two-minute demonstration (1991). Early in his career, Graves saw a need for longer (twenty- to thirty-minute) writing tutorials loaded with questions that teach. He recommended several question types for writing tutors (1983, 108–117):

Opening Questions

How is it going?

What are you writing about?

Where are you now in your draft?

Process Questions

What do you think you'll do next?

Where had you thought to start?

I notice that you changed your lead. It is much more direct. How did you do that?

If you were to put that new information in here, how would you go about doing it?

When you don't know how to spell a word, how do you go about figuring what to do?

What strategy do you use for figuring out where one sentence ends and the other one begins?

Among other tutor question types described by Graves are those that reveal development (by asking young writers how their work has changed over time), those that deal with basic structures (by asking writers to confront their understanding of information, revision, or writing standards), and those that challenge writers to become more self-sufficient beyond the tutorial. In the last decade or so, Graves has grown to prefer shorter writing conferences. He says that two-minute conferences can effectively fulfill the goals of writing tutorials.

One other area to which Graves has contributed significantly is in procedures for peer/small group writing tutorials. In setting up "writing share sessions," Graves (1994) suggests that three or four writers gather in a circle and take turns reading their papers aloud to each other. With each reading, the rest of the group listens carefully, then the group members tell the writer what they remember. Finally, the group members ask the writer one or two questions to learn more about the subject of the writing.

Muriel Harris

For writers at any age conference questions and dialogue contribute to their ability to become critics—and hence revisers—of their own work. (1985, 22)

For several years, Muriel Harris, a professor of English and the director of the Writing Lab at Purdue University, has been an enthusiastic champion of establishing writing tutorial centers in schools. She has taken a special interest in writing centers staffed by peer tutors, in the potential of tutor talk for building a writer's self-esteem, and in the array of roles writing tutors ought to be prepared to play.

Harris sees writing labs as special places because the tutorial interaction enriches the writer's academic experience and develops the writer's self-awareness in ways not possible in other institutionalized settings. Peer tutors add to the uniqueness of labs. Harris refers to the peer tutor as a "middle person" (1995) whose status is somewhere between the writer's and the teacher's and whose conversation with writers is often more free and honest than a teacher's would be. Peer writing tutors are unencumbered by grading pressure, attendance, assignments, tests, negative comments, and penalties for asking dumb questions.

Whether the tutor be a peer, a teacher or a parent, however, Harris emphasizes the power of talk to liberate the writer. Tutorial talk is not magical; it should consist of just "very normal conversations" (1985, 11). But these tutor/writer conversations lead to real gains in a writer's comfort level and confidence.

For a writer to achieve such affective boosts, collaboration between tutor and writer is a must:

> The most satisfying tutorials are those in which the students were active participants in finding their own criteria and solutions. (1995, 31)

One key for understanding the kind of collaboration that Harris promotes lies in her metaphor of tutor-as-coach (like Donald Murray's before her), in which the tutor works with a writer in much the same way a chef demonstrates processes in a cooking class or a tennis pro talks with a player as they practice together (1985). Within Harris' scheme, tutors-as-collaborators need to wear a few other hats in addition to that of coach:

> Tutor-as-commentator—gives the writer a larger perspective on what's going on.
>
> Tutor-as-counselor—considers the writer as a whole person
>
> Tutor-as-listener—attends to the developing meaning
>
> Tutor-as-diagnostician—points out problems in draft or process

Muriel Harris' work is extremely influential in all areas of tutoring writers, but especially in suggesting ways to improve the quality of talk between tutor and writer.

Walker Gibson

> So, I think I try to select, out of the thousands of things that would be possible to say, a couple of things that are really worth saying. Ideally, I'd love to make a connection between a critical remark of a general sort—voice or attitude—and specific matters of syntax. (1979a)

A longtime influence on the writing program at the University of Massachusetts at Amherst, where he is professor emeritus of English, Walker Gibson describes himself as "on the dramatistic side of the various arguments that go on in composition" (1979a). He believes that the practice of adopting a role as one writes is central, more interesting, and perhaps more teachable than matters of logic or organization are. In his tutorials, Gibson's absolutely key concern is voice.

In the late 1970s, Gibson encouraged two colleagues at UMass/Amherst to seek funding for National Endowment for the Humanities teacher institutes. The funding resulted in training for sixty Massachusetts secondary English teachers, all of whom spent time in a high school classroom that was taught with tutorial techniques like those used by Donald Murray and Roger Garrison (Moran 1994).

Although his writing conferences bear some resemblance to those of Murray and Garrison, Gibson puts his own stamp on the tutorial methodology by emphasizing the writer's attitude as it comes across in a paper. He asks questions like

Who is the writer?

What's her attitude?

And how is this affected by the audience?

In Gibson's tutorials, even syntax (for example, left-branching vs. right-branching sentences) is subjected to tests of tone. An especially useful quality of Gibson's tutorial style is that it shows writers how to detach themselves from their work and become "readers." This enables writers to uncover inconsistencies in voice, persona, and tone, as well as undesirable effects like sentimentality.

In Gibson's tutorials, LOCs and HOCs are strongly linked. A tutor's astute observation about a grammatical, punctuation, or syntactical concern often points the writer to a more significant—but clearly connected—high order deficiency in the writer's voice:

> I recall a really exciting conference I had . . . where I felt that a girl's position, or attitude, toward what she was talking about was somehow removed, distant, and almost stuffy. We did an analysis of one page in which we found something like fifteen verbs in the passive voice. Well, that was just wonderful, and by making those conversions, we changed the voice. So, it was a case where some of our thinking about grammar and some of our thinking about voice were identified, as they should be. (1979a)

In a tutorial with Chris, a college student, Gibson acts as a somewhat puzzled reader who is uncertain why he should be reading Chris' paper about James Joyce, which is meant to be a sketch for the *Encyclopaedia Britannica*: "Now tell me about the Joyce thing. Here what I worried about was audience. And, boy, did I fret about that, and I bet you did, too." Gibson reads the first sentence aloud and presses Chris to tinker with reshuffling the sentence in order to achieve her desired aim:

Gibson: We can just take the first sentence, maybe, and make something out of that. "On February 2, 1882, in Rathgar, Ireland, James Joyce was born." Is that the sentence structure of an *Encyclopaedia Britannica* article?

Chris: I would say so.

Gibson: Would you?

Chris: Well, maybe not an encyclopedia, but a history book on Joyce.

Gibson: Uh-huh. Maybe. What happens if we take the left-branching out? What happens then? "James Joyce was born on February 2, 1882, in Rathgar, Ireland." The tone changes enormously, doesn't it? We haven't changed a single word. All we've done is varied the order of the words and the tone is changed. Could you describe the difference? "James Joyce was born on February 2, 1881 . . ."

Chris: The second version seems more like it's more chronological order.

Gibson: Yes. I would argue that "James Joyce was born blah, blah, blah" is encyclopedia word order.

Gibson spends a few more minutes pointing out other places where problems at the sentence level distract the intended audience. Responding to one fragment error, Gibson says, "Now, I want you to change the subject just a little bit, and draw your attention to the third sentence. Now there, the voice suddenly falls apart. This is a very familiar example of what we call a sentence fragment and the result was a collapse in the voice."

Perhaps Gibson's signature as a supremely able writing tutor is his posture as a "dumb reader." He believes that by adopting the pose of a confused, bewildered reader, a tutor can help the writer comb through a paper for trouble spots. As the tutor reads a paper, she pauses whenever something in the text causes her discomfort or confusion. By engaging in this careful head-scratching or backtracking, the reader helps expose the features of a paper that fail to deliver the writer's intent. Eventually, by modeling a dumb reader, the tutor enables the writer to anticipate and prevent the need for "second perusals" by a baffled reader.

Gibson (1979b) cites a sentence written by one of his students that gave him an anxious moment as a dumb reader: "Though yesterday was really Tuesday, throughout the world it was Monday at the University of Massachusetts." Gibson's tutor-as-dumb reader stops and backtracks because of the misplaced comma:

> But I doubt that a review of comma rules will help this student. "Read the sentence aloud" is all I know to say to her. "Read it aloud and listen to yourself. Has your punctuation signal reflected your

own voice as it utters the sentence? Now what part of your sentence
does 'throughout the world' belong to?" (193)

Walker Gibson asks us as tutors to convince writers how easily and
often an attentive reader can go wrong. We can do that best by playing the role of "dumb reader."

Nancie Atwell

> The more I write, read about writing, respond to writers, and learn
> about each student, the more particular my conversations with my
> particular kids. I know that my conferences today are less ritualized
> and formulaic than when I began teaching writing in a workshop
> because my knowledge base has broadened and deepened. I've gone
> from acting as a mirror, someone who reflects back what I hear in
> the writing and gives a neutral response, to trying to act as a mentor
> to young writers. (1998, 229–230)

As a seventh- and eighth-grade teacher at the school she founded in
Maine, the Center for Teaching and Learning, Nancie Atwell epito-
mizes a master tutor evolving in her craft. She doesn't hesitate to be
more authoritarian and directive in tutorials with adolescent writers:
"Sometimes in conferences I intervene to nudge a writer to a place he
or she hasn't been and needs to go in order to grow" (1998, 242).
Atwell's goal is to "act as a good parent," as a "grown-up writer who
listens to kids and shows kids how it's done, gives sound advice, and
convinces them she knows what she's talking about" (21).

It's a tricky balancing act: Youngsters want to be listened to, but
at the same time they want honest response from adults. Atwell outlines things to do when tutoring young writers who have a draft,
including these:

- Build on what writers know and have done, rather than concen-
  trating on negatives.
- Ask questions about something in the paper that piques your
  curiosity.
- Come to each session equipped with a pad of sticky notes and use
  it to jot down on-the-spot questions and comments so that they
  won't be lost.

For Atwell, a typical one-to-one conversation about the writer's content and craft follows this routine:

1. The tutor invites the writer to talk.
2. The writer talks.

3. The tutor listens.

4. The tutor paraphrases, asks questions, suggests alternatives as the writer needs them, and asks about the writer's plans.

An ingenious invention of Atwell's is her notion of writers tutoring themselves. When Atwell found that students weren't reading their own work-in-progress, she constructed an in-depth guide called "Having a Writing Conference with Yourself" (1998) for students to consult. Although many of the questions could be used by tutors, Atwell's list is designed chiefly for young writers to refer to as they read their own writing to themselves. They ask themselves questions about their purpose, information, leads, conclusions, titles, and style.

Peter Elbow

> Writing is a string you send out to connect yourself with other consciousnesses, but usually you never have the opportunity to feel anything at the other end. How can you tell whether you've got a fish if the line always feels slack? . . . To improve your writing you don't need advice about what changes to make; you don't need theories of what is good and bad writing. You need movies of people's minds while they read your words. (1973)

Nearly thirty years ago, Peter Elbow, now a professor of English at the University of Massachusetts at Amherst, conceived of a self-help book for writers. In one chapter of the 1973 work, "The Teacherless Writing Class," he describes several innovative ways that writers in small groups can give quality response to each other. Each of Elbow's classic methods can easily be adapted to a tutor/writer interaction. There is no set structure or sequence to the approaches, and tutors may pick and choose from among them to help writers revise.

- Movies of the Reader's Mind: The tutor tells the writer frankly what happens inside her mind as she reads the writer's words.

- Pointing: The tutor shares with the writer which phrases or words stick in her mind and which passages or features she likes best.

- Center of Gravity: The tutor summarizes in a single sentence what she sees as the source of energy, the focal point, the nutshell idea for the paper.

- Believing and Doubting: The tutor first is asked to believe (or pretend to believe) everything the writer has produced and to tell the writer (as an advocate) what she sees (offering the writer more ideas that would help the writer's case). Then, the tutor switches stances and doubts everything, tells the writer what she sees, and offers arguments against what the writer has presented.

- Sayback: In her own words, the tutor tells the writer what she heard the writer getting at in the paper.

- What is Almost Said: The tutor lets the writer know what is implied or hovering around the edges of the paper and what she would like to hear more about.

The underlying principle in Elbow's response mechanism is that the tutor/respondent supports the writer's work rather than judging it.

Thomas Newkirk

> First I read the paper. Then, as a kind of probe, to see what kind of need the student has in the paper, the student tells what needs to be done. Usually, they'll say something and we might talk about that. Then, I'll have a reaction to the paper. (1979a)

Tom Newkirk's special brand of writing tutorial is characterized by a fast-paced informality that makes it seem more like a chat than a formal one-to-one instructional session. However, there is a definite structure to Newkirk's tutoring. He suggests groups of questions that tutors might ask for discovery, for arrangement, and for language and style, all the while cautioning tutors that realistically they may end up dealing with only one or two questions per conference (1979b). Here's a sampling of Newkirk's orderly parade of tutor questions:

Questions for Discovery

1. What is working?
2. At what points does the paper need more detail?
3. Is the paper sufficiently complex? Are important alternatives explored? Questions answered?

Questions for Arrangement

1. What has been improved?
2. Does the beginning begin the piece?
3. Does the ending end it?
4. Are there any weak sections that can be eliminated?

Questions for Style and Language

1. Are there sentences that could be profitably combined?
2. Is the movement from sentence to sentence clear?

Newkirk (1979a) reaffirms his belief in the prioritized pattern of question-asking that tutors can follow by relying on the metaphor of tutor-as-camera:

> I compare it to a camera. First the wide angle: You're not looking just at the paper, but you are trying to sense everything around the paper. Then the second reading you focus on the outlines of the paper, talking about arrangement within that frame. The frame has been decided on the second reading. The third reading you are looking telescopically in the frame at parts within the frame. In the third reading it doesn't make any difference if you finish the paper, because you just want to find a pattern of syntactic errors. (5)

A final service that Newkirk renders for the world of writing tutorials is to remind us of the critical importance of the first few moments of a one-to-one session. The first five or so minutes give the conference a sense of direction and establish the agenda. Newkirk urges us to invite writer input from the outset of a conference so that the tutorial has a "mutually agreeable and mutually understood direction" (1989, 328). He warns against tutors fixing on a problem and setting their own agenda too early, thus missing opportunities for the writer's contribution to the dialectic encounter.

Chapter Ten

Tutoring and Technology

Tutoring by its very nature shows writers that writing is a process of collaboration and revision. In tutoring, this collaboration usually takes place face-to-face across a table, desk, or even the arm of a comfy chair. But the collaborative nature of tutoring allows it to occur in other ways, especially ways that are supported by electronic communication technologies. These technologies extend the spatial and time dimensions of tutoring so that it can occur between people who are separated by great distances and between people who dialogue at times that are convenient for them. This chapter discusses how electronic communication technologies can be used in tutoring. For a list of related resources, see "Electronic Resources" at the back of this book.

Electronic communication technologies reduce the face-to-face interaction, the most complex and informative type of tutoring, to interaction that uses just the human voice or just the piece of writing itself. Face-to-face is the preferred method of tutoring not only because it keeps the human elements at maximum but also because all the research that supports tutoring assumed face-to-face tutoring; therefore, face-to-face is the only mode that has a fully developed research ground. But electronic communication technologies offer a generally theoretically sound medium for tutoring, even if it is not yet grounded in research. Using technologies allows the expansion of the time and space of tutoring, making tutoring available to writers, even if in a reduced form, in ways that blend with many people's writing processes and lives.

Telephone

One of the simplest and most frequent uses of technology for tutoring has been available for years—telephone someone to talk about something you're writing. Whether it's Hemingway calling his New York City editor from Key West or an office worker calling the person down the hall, a telephone chat about a developing piece of writing can be a valuable tutoring experience.

Tutoring by telephone can support something that's recognized as a behavior of successful and effective writers: looking at the writing at a global level. While good writers regularly evaluate their work at the level of the whole, weaker writers too often neglect this level in favor of focusing on particular parts of the work. In a telephone tutoring situation, only the writer can see the draft. The writer must establish a context for the tutor by describing the piece at the global or macro level.

Of course, many other levels of a piece of writing can be discussed on the phone, from the micro focus of punctuation to the medium focus of the development or ordering of paragraphs, and more. Tutoring requires that the writer verbalize problems in the piece, which is useful because the very act of verbalizing can clarify the exact nature of a problem that, without verbalizing, may have remained foggy. Tutoring by telephone requires that the writer do maximum verbalization, thus supporting behaviors that are associated with effective composing processes and tutoring sessions.

Every tutor who works by phone—a tutor at a writing center that has a call-in writing problems hotline; an office worker who is responsible for supporting writing in her work group; a parent at work whose child calls with a writing problem—should be encouraged to make the telephone do its thing by prompting the writer to pop up and look at the global level of the piece, or by asking questions that require the writer to verbalize the problem. Both strategies maximize how the telephone can be used to support the behaviors of successful writers.

Fax

One way that a writer and tutor who are separated can share a piece of writing is to fax it back and forth. The advantages of faxing include the speed at which drafts can be exchanged and the fact that writer and tutor can look at faxes in either electronic or paper form. If the fax is exchanged as an electronic draft, then writers and tutors can proceed as they would if it had been exchanged by e-mail or the World Wide Web. Printing out drafts has certain advantages: A printout will show actual annotations made to a piece, so writers and tutors can draw arrows and write between lines or in margins. The e-mail and word processing software used to exchange electronic drafts may or may not support annotating; paper faxes allow this more graphic type of response, which can facilitate the writer's ability to see problems and begin to understand potential revisions.

When writer and tutor exchange paper faxes, they should allow the fax technology to do its thing by using graphic and locational strategies to the maximum. We expect that tutors will understand the use of arrows, circles, carets, and some proofreading symbols. We recommend that they add to this repertoire a fair number of journalistic proofreading and editing symbols, and that they use shading and highlighting to point things out to their fax partner. If color fax machines are available at both ends, color can be used to show things in the draft. Paper fax allows for an interface between graphics and response to writing. And, a point not to be missed, it also allows for a more human connection between writer and tutor than other means of electronic tutoring do, since handwriting and drawing are expressions of self that are missing in the mostly electronic world of communication technology.

E-mail and the Web

E-mail is probably the most frequent form of electronic tutoring simply because colleges, school districts, most workplaces, and many homes are wired for e-mail. The process of e-mailing is known to many students and, if not, is easy to learn, especially in newer World Wide Web–based systems that have user-friendly mouse- and icon-based operations. Tutoring using e-mail is an easy to understand process: The writer sends her draft and questions and comments to the tutor; the tutor responds to the draft and the questions and comments. E-mail allows both tutor and writer to insert questions or comments right in the draft to pinpoint problem places, or to place more lengthy responses at the end. Alternately, questions and comments can appear in the e-mail message while the actual draft is attached to the message as an electronic file. However the piece and the questions and comments are exchanged, tutors and writers are able to create the writing and reflection that are essential to successful tutoring.

Tutors must establish a few rules for e-mail exchanges that make tutors' and writers' words distinguishable. In our sessions, tutors use ALL CAPS. E-mail programs don't necessarily read bold or italics, but they all read caps. This allows the writer to go the easier route of using the word processing program's standard font. Because tutors often read a draft, then scan it to find inserted questions and comments to which they need to respond, questions or comments inserted into the draft go between <arrowheads>, which are easier to spot in text than [brackets] or {braces} are.

The basic e-mail tutoring scenario assumes that writer and tutor take turns e-mailing back and forth, with each checking for a new message when their schedule allows. This is one of the great advantages of much electronic communication technology—it can fit students', workers', and parents' schedules. But e-mail does not have to be done in this asynchronous, turn-taking fashion. Many e-mail programs allow for synchronous chat or nearly simultaneous dialogue. Writer and tutor can discuss a draft as two polite conversers who do not interrupt each other, but who respond immediately when the other finishes typing. This step-by-step dialogue is a lot like a spoken conversation. The draft itself can be shared in its own e-mail or attached after revision.

Specialized networked software called "groupware" is designed so that multiple users can work on the same document at the same time. This lets the tutor respond or question during drafting or revision. It's even possible for multiple writers and multiple tutors to interact in synchronous dialogue. Unfortunately, such synchronous group activity is available only on networked systems, not between systems on e-mail, so it's most likely to occur in colleges, schools, and workplaces.

The Internet does allow for synchronous writing, so writers who are not directly networked as in classroom, college, or office can still have synchronous exchanges. One type of Internet software allows for synchronous chat to be displayed at high speed (Instant Messaging, for example). Tutors, whether based in writing centers, classrooms, offices, or homes, could use this software to talk to a writer or group of writers about writing, authors, or a specific draft that had been shared by e-mail. Another type of Internet software, called *MUDs* and later *MOOs* in computerese, allows writers and tutors to connect synchronously in a virtual classroom or writing center and work collaboratively on writing while discussing the process and the developing product. Writing teachers and writing center staff are already using MOOs to connect across grades and geographical distances, which makes getting responses to writing convenient.

Tutoring Using Online Writing Labs

Online writing labs (OWLs) are websites designed to support writers' processes and products by supplying easy access to electronic writing resources and online tutoring. Most OWLs are associated with either two- or four-year college writing centers, although a few are sponsored by and aimed at secondary schools. Public adult literacy programs may also begin to develop OWLs or even OLLs (online literacy labs), since many of the larger such programs already sponsor telephone hotlines or newspaper columns that give writing advice (for example, the Pittsburgh Literacy Council sponsors a grammar advice column in the *Pittsburgh Post-Gazette*). We know of no OWLs that are sponsored by or aimed at the workplace or the home, although workplace and home tutors can easily access the OWLs currently on the Web since they are free and open to the public. Of course, when a college's OWL is asked to respond to a document from the workplace or a paper from a homeschooled secondary student, the college will have to decide just how far its sense of community service extends.

Tutoring through OWLs generally works like tutoring done through e-mail or other Internet connections, with the addition of a few unique features. Most OWLs have online resources, often called "handouts," and links to other writing-related websites. Where these resources and links are present, they can be used in the tutoring process as the tutor and writer see fit.

OWL handouts are specifically designed explanations and examples of writing problems and possible solutions or strategies to eliminate them. Tutors can discuss pieces of writing or writing problems with an eye to using specific handouts for each writer. A tutoring session might consist of a discussion between tutor and writer; a break while the writer reviews one or more handouts; then another connection in which tutor and writer discuss the issues the writer has just reviewed.

For example, the Purdue University Online Writing Lab (http://owl.english.purdue.edu) offers 130 handouts ranging across such topics as sentence construction, writing research papers and citing sources, spelling, and writing in the job search. Topics are grouped into subcategories that are in turn part of larger categories. For example, the larger General Writing Concerns category groups handouts in these useful and important subcategories, all of which are regular concerns in tutoring:

Planning/Starting to Write—includes Asking the Right Questions when you start to write

Style/Clarity/Coherence—includes Transitions, Adding Emphasis, Eliminating Wordiness

Revising/Editing/Proofreading—includes HOCs and LOCs, Steps in Editing, Proofreading Strategies

Effective Writing—includes Coping with Writing Anxiety,

Overcoming Writer's Block

Other Issues/Topics—includes Non-Sexist Language, Logic in Argumentative Writing, Writing Essay Exams

Tutors can use all these handouts to create an individualized instructional process.

Tutors can also use the OWL's links to other websites that would be appropriate for the writer to visit and review. A tutoring session might include discussion interspersed with linking to other writing sites.

For example, the University of Missouri's Online Writery (http://web.missouri.edu/~writery), offers a variety of links to other websites of significance, grouped as follows:

General Resources—includes Writer's Block Bulletin Board System (a virtual community for writers), Writer's Resources on the Web, The Playwright's Project

Authors and Online Writing—includes Writers on the Net (online classes, tutoring, mentoring, and writers' groups), Seamus Heaney Cover Page, Columbia Journalism Review Homepage

Online Writing Labs—includes the University of Maine (descriptions of other OWLs), National Writing Centers Association (writing centers, tutor stories, writing center start-up kit)

Publishing—includes Publishers' Catalogues Home Page

Children's—includes Children's Writing Resource Center

In addition to the handouts and links that characterize most OWLs, many also have references to and abstracts of recommendations for writing instructors and tutor trainers from recent theory, research, and pedagogy. These professional resources are sometimes supplemented by writing and tutoring training course syllabi; for writing teachers, tutor trainers, tutors, and writing center staff, this rich variety of resources makes visiting several OWLs worth the time it takes.

Chapter Eleven

A Tutor Training Course

This chapter provides concrete guidelines for formally preparing writing tutors in a training course. For college writing center directors, the course would run for fifteen weeks—the typical length of a college semester. For other tutor trainers—coordinators of basic skills centers that provide individualized help to secondary school writers, leaders of community literacy organizations, and supervisors of workplace staff writing development programs—the training period and curriculum will vary according to need.

This fifteen-week course syllabus includes week-by-week activities, ways for tutors to document their interactions with writers, and evaluation schemes for monitoring and judging the tutor/writer transaction. These components could be chosen among and adapted to create a course as short as one day.

A course like this ought to be writing-intensive. That is, in addition to being trained in tutoring techniques and interacting one-to-one with writers, students in the course should do an ample amount of writing themselves. As a former student of ours put it, after finishing a tutor training course: "I've learned how my writing process really works by trying to explain things to a student. In responding to needs of students I discovered my own needs."

Course Syllabus

Texts

- Elbow, P. 1998. *Writing with Power.* New York: Oxford University Press.

- McAndrew, D., & T. Reigstad 2001. *Tutoring Writers*. Portsmouth, NH: Boynton/Cook.
- Murray, D. 1985. *A Writer Teaches Writing*. Boston: Houghton Mifflin

Prerequisite

- Student tutors should have fulfilled basic college composition requirements.

Course Objectives

- Tutors will understand writing as a process of discovery and investigation as well as a mode of communication.
- Tutors will view conferring with writers as an important mode of writing instruction.
- Tutors will gain insight into the composing processes of writers in general, and of inexperienced writers in particular.
- Tutors will become more aware of their own composing processes.
- Tutors will learn several tutoring strategies available to them when conferring with writers and will apply them during conferences.
- Tutors will gain insight into techniques that may help them improve their own writing.
- Tutors will learn how to diagnose writing problems.
- Tutors will understand the importance of establishing a supportive rapport with writers during conferences.
- Tutors will become aware that writers' native use of dialect or a language other than English creates special writing problems, and will learn to apply specific tutoring techniques to meet these writers' special needs.
- Tutors will learn how to use the power of computers and the Internet to assist their responses to writers.

Course Requirements and Policies

To earn a grade of C, tutors must

a. Attend and participate in all class sessions.

b. Report for all tutoring hours.

c. Satisfactorily complete all class assignments and readings.

d. Choose five readings from the reserve material and write a one- or two-page reaction paper for each, based on the piece and on the tutor's experiences with tutoring.

To earn a grade of B, tutors must complete requirements a, b, and c and

e. Choose ten readings from the reserve material and write a one- or two-page reaction paper for each, based on the piece and on the tutor's experiences with tutoring.

f. Maintain a journal that includes comments on tutoring experiences and reflections.

To earn a grade of A, tutors must complete requirements a, b, c, e, and f and

g. Write a five-to-seven-page case study report based on the tutor's work with one writer over time.

Course Outline

Week 1

- Students complete the Writing Attitude Scale shown in Figure 11–1 (pretraining measurement).
- Students complete a writing sample (pretraining measurement).
- Instructor explains the composing process (McAndrew and Reigstad Chapter 4; Murray Chapters 1–3).

Week 2

- Students compose drafts of Paper 1: "How I Write."
- Instructor and students discuss the composing process in connection with these drafts.
- Instructor explains positive rapport and positive paper comments with reference to the Tutor Critique Sheet (Figure 11–2).
- Instructor explains related theory and research (McAndrew and Reigstad Chapters 1–2).
- Students use their drafts of Paper 1 to complete items 1 and 2 on the Tutor Critique Sheet.

Week 3

- Instructor explains the tutoring process and the priority of concerns, introducing the idea of HOCs and LOCs (McAndrew and Reigstad Chapters 3–4; Murray Chapters 6–8).

Figure 11–1
The Scale Used to Assess Attitudes Toward Writing
Before and After Training

Writing Attitude Scale

There are no right or wrong responses to the following statements about writing. Please indicate as honestly as possible how you feel about each statement on the scale provided.

5=strongly agree; 4=agree; 3=uncertain; 2=disagree; 1=strongly disagree

1 2 3 4 5   1. I look forward to writing down my own ideas.

1 2 3 4 5   2. I have no fear of my writing being evaluated.

1 2 3 4 5   3. I hate writing.

1 2 3 4 5   4. If I have something to express, I'd rather write it than say it.

1 2 3 4 5   5. I am afraid of writing when I know what I write will be evaluated.

1 2 3 4 5   6. My mind usually seems to go blank when I start to work on a composition.

1 2 3 4 5   7. Expressing my ideas through writing seems to be a waste of time.

1 2 3 4 5   8. I don't like my compositions to be evaluated.

1 2 3 4 5   9. I see writing as having no more value than other forms of communication.

1 2 3 4 5   10. I feel confident in my ability to express my ideas clearly in writing.

1 2 3 4 5   11. I see writing as an outdated, useless way of communicating.

1 2 3 4 5   12. In my major or in the field of my future occupation, writing is an enjoyable experience.

1 2 3 4 5   13. I seem to be able to write down my ideas clearly.

1 2 3 4 5   14. Writing is a beneficial skill.

1 2 3 4 5   15. Discussing my writing with others is an enjoyable experience.

1 2 3 4 5   16. I have a terrible time organizing my ideas in an essay.

1 2 3 4 5   17. When I have something to express, I'd rather say it than write it.

1 2 3 4 5   18. An ability to write will be worthwhile in my occupation.

1 2 3 4 5   19. I enjoy writing.

1 2 3 4 5   20. I'm no good at writing.

Figure 11–2
The Form Used by Tutors to Record In-Class
Critiques of Student Writing

Tutor Critique Sheet

1. Make a positive, rapport-creating statement to the writer.

2. Make two positive comments about the paper. What are its strengths?

3. Describe any weakness you find in the areas listed below. Suggest a strategy to eliminate each weakness. Record your comments below.
   a. thesis or focus
   b. voice or tone
   c. organization
   d. development

4. List any weaknesses you see in sentence structure, punctuation, usage, and spelling. Suggest a strategy to eliminate each weakness. Record your comments below.

- Instructor explains and illustrates the first HOC (thesis/focus) and strategies for improvement.
- Students complete drafts for Paper 2 (reaction paper #1) and fill in items 1–3a on the Tutor Critique Sheets for Papers 1 and 2.

Week 4

- Instructor explains and illustrates the second HOC (voice/tone) and strategies for improvement (Murray Chapter 10).
- Students complete drafts for Paper 3 (reaction paper) and fill in items 1–3b on the Tutor Critique Sheets for Papers 1–3.

Week 5

- Students complete drafts of Paper 4 and items 1–3c on the Tutor Critique Sheets for Papers 1–4.
- Instructor explains and illustrates the fourth HOC (development) and strategies for improvement.
- Students complete drafts of Paper 5 and items 1–3d on the Tutor Critique Sheets for Papers 1–5.

Week 6

- Instructor explains and illustrates LOCs and strategies for improvement.

Figure 11–3

Worksheet for Evaluating Three Tutorial Options

Tutoring Option Worksheet

	Student-Centered	Collaborative	Teacher-Oriented
1. Note instances when the tutor switches from talking directly about the paper to talking about other subjects.			
2. Record the types of questions by placing a check in the appropriate row each time the tutor asks a question. a. closed: has only one answer b. open: has many possible answers c. leading: has an answer already known by the tutor d. probing: helps the student see possibilities e. yes/no: requires only a yes or no answer			
3. Describe the climate of the tutoring session. Choose one word from each pair. a. conversational/lecture-like b. warm/cool c. student/teacher d. mutual effort/individual effort			
4. Indicate who talked the most. Choose one. a. tutor b. student c. equal			
5. Indicate what was discussed. Choose as many as apply. a. thesis or focus b. voice or tone c. organization d. development e. lower order concerns			

- Students complete drafts of Paper 6 and items 1–4 on the Tutor Critique Sheets for Papers 1–6.
- Instructor and students discuss the tutoring model and lessons gained from highly regarded writing tutors (McAndrew and Reigstad Chapters 6 and 9).
- Tutorial sessions (in classrooms or writing centers) commence.

Week 7

- Instructor evaluates student skills with HOCs and LOCs by discussing their completed Tutor Critique Sheets.
- Instructor and students discuss the importance of body language, tone of voice, and the tutoring environment.
- Instructor explains ways to tutor writers who present challenges because they are ESL learners or because of their gender, learning styles, or ability level (McAndrew and Reigstad Chapters 4 and 8).

Week 8

- Instructor explains and illustrates tutor questions and prewriting techniques for helping writers without a draft (Elbow Chapters 2 and 3; McAndrew and Reigstad Chapter 5).
- Instructor presents three options for tutorial interaction: student-centered, collaborative, and teacher-oriented.
- Instructor demonstrates or shows videotapes of the three tutorial options; students practice identifying features of each option, using the Tutoring Option Worksheet (Figure 11–3).
- Students complete drafts of Paper 7 and use them to role-play the three tutorial options.

Week 9

- Instructor explains record keeping (Figures 11–4 through 11–6).
- Instructor shows how computers can be a rich resource for writing tutors (McAndrew and Reigstad Chapter 10).
- Students observe a demonstration or a videotaped tutorial session based on a draft that has been reproduced and distributed to the class.

Week 10

- Students critique the demonstration or videotape, using the Tutoring Option Worksheet.
- Students complete drafts of Paper 8 and use them to role-play tutoring sessions.
- Instructor and students critique the role-playing sessions.

Figure 11–4
A Log Sheet Filled Out by Writing Tutors

Writing Tutor Log Sheet
(Please fill out after each session and leave in folder)

Tutor: _____   Date: _____

Writer: _____

We Worked On   FOCUS

_____   A) Formulate a thesis

_____   B) Write to/for a specific audience

_____   C) Use more exact words and expressions

ORGANIZATION

_____   D) Use transitions

_____   E) Present an intro, body & conclusion

_____   F) Divide information into paragraphs

DEVELOPMENT

_____   G) Use a topic sentence in each paragraph

_____   H) Relate paragraphs to focus of paper

_____   I) Use appropriate details to develop ideas

MECHANICS/EDITING

_____   J) Eliminate run-ons and fragments

_____   K) Make subject and verb agree

_____   L) Keep verb tense consistent

_____   M) Use pronouns correctly

_____   N) Spell correctly

_____   O) Use other punctuation properly

_____   BRAINSTORMING

COMMENTS:

Figure 11–5
Writing Tutor Observation Form

Writing Tutor's Name: _____ Date of Tutoring Session: _____

Observer: _____

	Strongly Agree	Agree	Disagree	Strongly Disagree
1. The tutor is polite and courteous.	_____	_____	_____	_____
2. The tutor makes positive comments about the paper.	_____	_____	_____	_____
3. The tutor appears interested and is not preoccupied with other work.	_____	_____	_____	_____
4. The tutor explains things clearly and in a way that the writer understands.	_____	_____	_____	_____
5. The tutor establishes a good rapport with the writer.	_____	_____	_____	_____
6. The tutor asks questions.	_____	_____	_____	_____
7. The tutor uses restatements to aid the writer in rethinking her work.	_____	_____	_____	_____
8. The tutor allows for a period of wait time after asking the writer a question or after the writer speaks.	_____	_____	_____	_____
9. The tutor allows the writer to set the agenda.	_____	_____	_____	_____
10. The tutor makes good use of available conference time.	_____	_____	_____	_____
11. The tutor provides closure and an invitation to visit again.	_____	_____	_____	_____

Figure 11–6
Form for Writer to Evaluate Tutoring Session

Writer's Evaluation of Tutoring Session

Date: _____

* QUALITY OF TUTORING: Do you feel the tutoring you received was appropriate, clear and effectively presented?

1	2	3	4	5
not clear & ineffective		adequate		very clear & very effective

* QUALITY OF TUTOR: Do you feel that the tutor you worked with was helpful and competent?

1	2	3	4	5
incompetent		adequate		very helpful & very competent

* WRITING PROGRESS: Do you feel that you made progress with your piece of writing (or with your writing problem) as a result of the tutoring session?

1	2	3	4	5
no progress		some progress		much progress

CHECK THE WORDS THAT BEST DESCRIBE YOUR TUTOR:

___ approachable	___ poor listener	___ interested
___ annoyed	___ good listener	___ helpful
___ impatient	___ friendly	___ prepared
___ ineffective	___ effective	___ not prepared
___ not helpful	___ uninterested	___ patient

___ other (specify) _____

Weeks 11–14

- Students continue tutoring writers.
- Instructor monitors quality of tutorial sessions.

Week 15

- Students complete the Writing Attitude Scale (posttraining measurement).
- Students complete a writing sample (posttraining measurement).

Comments on Course Features

Whatever the boundaries of the schedule (fifteen weeks, four weeks, one week), the growth in writing ability of the tutors-in-training should be measured; so should changes in their attitude toward writing. We use the Writing Attitude Scale (Figure 11–1) to assess change in the affective domain and a writing sample to assess change in writing ability. The scale, derived in part from John Daly and Michael Miller (1975), consists of twenty statements to which students react. To score the attitude scale, add all scores for statements 1, 2, 4, 10, 12, 13, 14, 15,18, 19 (maximum score 50) and subtract all scores for the other statements: [positive scores] – [negative scores] = attitude. A person who has an extremely positive attitude toward writing should score a plus 40, and a person who has an extremely negative attitude should score a minus 40. (Test results may be more accurate if you cover up the positive and negative indicators when you copy this scale for your students).

Growth in positive attitude toward writing is shown by a positive difference between pretraining and posttraining evaluations. The writing ability measurement is based on paired papers written at the beginning and at the end of the course in response to prompts of similar difficulty. Each student's papers are given a "pick-the-better" rating by two or three raters. The posttraining paper should be consistently chosen as the better, otherwise there has been little growth in writing ability.

It is important to emphasize that students should not begin tutoring until they are prepared to do so. Although some tutor trainers (Bruffee 1980) encourage more immediate tutoring, we believe that a writer who experiences a tutoring session that is ineffective because the tutor isn't prepared is not likely to participate again. Therefore, in a fifteen-week course, we recommend that students begin tutoring concurrently with course business no earlier than the fourth week.

Course Features

The "How I Write" Paper

Early in the course students compose a paper that describes their own writing processes, habits, and rituals. Students should be told that their audience is their fellow tutors-in-training in the class, not just the instructor. Provide a list of prompts like these:

When do you get the urge to write?

Under what circumstances does writing become easier (or more difficult)?

What do you find most enjoyable (or most unpleasant) about writing?

Can you think of any quirks or gimmicks you use to get started, to keep going, or to finish up?

What is an ideal writing situation for you (for instance, what things do you like to have around)?

Do you ever think of who will read your writing?

An alternative for this assignment would be to ask students to recall a paper that they recently completed and to write up a blow-by-blow account of how they composed it. Christopher Scanlan (1983) has edited a fascinating collection of published pieces of newswriting and the authors' firsthand looks at how they wrote the stories. Any one of the "story/how I wrote it" entries in his book could provide useful models for students. Another model, shown in Figure 11–7, is Maryanne Reigstad's "How I Wrote the Story," which gives insight into a profile she published in the November 2, 1985, issue of *Business First of Buffalo*, a local business weekly newspaper.

Keeping a Tutoring Journal

We ask students to jot down impressions and observations of their tutoring experience in a journal as the course unfolds. These notes can be informal. They can be impromptu or reflective. They can predict what might happen before a tutorial session or comment on how the session went. They can include fragmentary notes and artifacts (scraps of conversation or drafts) salvaged from the tutorial meetings. The entries can focus inward on the tutor's thoughts and outward on the writer's behavior and response. They should be written in regular installments throughout the course. The main goal is to encourage tutors to capture insights into their tutoring experience that might

Figure 11–7
Maryanne Reigstad's "How I Wrote the Story" Account

How I Wrote the Story

The profile on Herbert Lustig talked about an issue of general interest through an individual. While it was personal and singular, it was also extensive. It gave a local perspective on a national topic through the eyes and experience of someone who has played the role at both levels.

Interviewing Lustig was immensely interesting, his professional views peppered with personal glimpses. It was impressive to hear him speak with such knowledge about a complex issue and still be able to get his message across in regular English.

One of the overriding personal traits that came across during the interview was Lustig's energy, which was conveyed through his animated style of conversation. To derive the lead, I reviewed my notes and reflected a lot about how Lustig behaved and looked, how he talked, moved, how he kept his office. During the interview, I asked him how he felt about Buffalo, having been raised in New York City, how he spent his free time, and what principles he lived by that he also applied in his work—conversational things that I usually ask to give insight into a person's character and that can be used to give texture to a story. It turned out that Lustig is an avid race-walker. You know how energetic and wiry those guys are. Although I didn't use those facts in the story, they led me to see this energy—obviously a plus if you're a litigation attorney. In recalling the interview, I envisioned the sky outside the window: grey and blah. Quite a contrast to the energy of the man in the office. I thought that contrast would make a good lead.

When I got the assignment, it was given in rather general terms but was supposed to have been a focus on the man. However, it was hard to separate the subject matter—liability—and the man. So it turned into a piece with a dual nature. Fortunately, it was allowed to evolve that way because the original story on the liability insurance crisis fell through, and the profile was used as the lead story for the special report section.

---

otherwise have been lost or forgotten, and to have them engage in continuous self-assessment. If journals are to be graded, we suggest using three criteria recommended by Randy Bomer (1995): the volume of entries; the variety of entries (entries cover many facets of tutoring); and the thoughtfulness of entries.

Here's a sample entry from college student Gabriel's tutoring journal describing a weekly encounter with two tenth-grade high school English students, Matt and Adam:

> 3/16 Read Matt's next-to-final draft. Pretty good. He has it documented the way the teacher wants it. Not the way I would have told

Figure 11–8
Tom's Case Study of Tutoring Cynthia

I was lucky to tutor Cynthia, a conscientious and determined student. She came every week, she did her assignments, and she improved dramatically.

Although Cynthia had an honest desire to improve her writing, she had a more important goal. She was a student in English 102, and it was not her first encounter with that course. She had failed the exam the previous semester.

In many ways her writing was good, especially her tone—friendly, unpretentious—but it also suffered from wordiness, vagueness, and mostly prepositions. I couldn't believe that someone could string so many of them so easily into such giant behemoths. Attached is the first essay I read. One sentence contained 46 words, another 38, and within each, prepositions were the main connectors. For example, in the first sentence, a sentence of only 23 words—one of her shortest—there were 5 prepositions. That's not so bad but in the third paragraph's lead sentence there were 8, and that's a heavy load for any sentence to carry. The problem was that the prepositions scattered the strength of her arguments since they allowed her to harbor information in one sentence that should have been housed in several. In fact the entire essay consisted of only 8 sentences so that reading it was like being mired in an endless swamp of words with no one there to give me directions.

You had recommended the student-centered approach, so I began our first session by asking her questions. I discovered that she wrote long sentences whenever she didn't understand the topic because she hoped that her complicated sentences would obscure that fact. I suggested that she highlight the readings given to her, so she'd be better prepared. She promised to give it a try. I also suggested that she learn many of the prepositions by heart so that she'd be better aware of them in her writing and might avoid them. Lastly I offered her alternatives—other connectors like relative pronouns, conjunctions, and the semi-colon.

Another early question was why she began the three paragraphs with "In discussing . . . ," "In looking at . . ." And "In discussing . . ." She admitted a fear of writing simple sentences. She believed that her ideas would seem simple as well. I told her that short sentences are clearer, easier for the reader to digest. Further, variation in sentence length—mixture of long and short sentences—makes one's writing flow more smoothly. Lastly I reminded her that if she were better prepared, she wouldn't need to hide her unfamiliarity with a topic. Our first few sessions were spent with my asking questions and making a few suggestions. But I didn't see any progress, so against your instructions, I admit, I began taking the directive approach.

I began by looking at her essays with my pen in hand. Usually what I did was underline the prepositions and read the sentences aloud to her, so she'd

continued

Figure 11–8, continued

be aware of their sing-song rhythm. Also I read aloud her longer sentences and showed her how they could be dissected into smaller ones. After a few sessions, she'd smile and say, "Ah, you're gonna be picky again"—and I was. I always told her what I liked, but I also told her what I disliked. I knew the test was approaching and she needed to make a lot of progress in a little time.

The prepositions slowly retreated from her writing, but where she didn't make progress was sentence beginnings. I told her at first that she could begin with a dependent clause instead of a prepositional phrase. That, she accepted. But later I had to make her promise to write just one simple sentence beginning with "The." You'd have thought I was killing her.

Although you had recommended the "aluminum" exercise, I didn't think it would help since she didn't need to lengthen sentences, she needed to shorten them. Then you gave me the exercises for controlling sprawl, and I decided to use both the "aluminum" and "chicken" exercises combined with the ones for controlling sprawl so that she'd have practice putting sentences together and taking them apart. Attached is the "aluminum" exercise. I saw considerable improvement.

Although many sentences were too short, for her it was an excellent exercise—short sentences and few prepositions. The only negative comment I had concerned her handwriting. Many letters which looked like capitals weren't, and her commas looked like periods. I worried that someone grading her test would confuse them and would consequently fail her.

I continued giving her exercises, which she worked at conscientiously. Finally as the test approached, her professor began grading their exams 102 ("failing") or Exempt. Attached is the first of these. It was graded Exempt.

Some of the old problems still persisted. There were no particularly short sentences and prepositions still thrived. Nevertheless the sentences were shorter, the prepositions fewer. In fact she began the first sentence with "The." I was impressed.

With the test near, I urged her to outline several essays before class, which she did. My biggest concern then was not sentence length or prepositions, though both could have stood further improvement. I worried about capitalization and punctuation. Some lower case letters still looked like capitals and her commas like periods.

My last concern, though, was whether my "pickiness" had made her feel more insecure, so I gave her the attitude scale. I was surprised—she had a better attitude than I did. When we left our last session, I was confident that she would pass. I liked Cynthia a lot. We had grown to be friends, and I had an emotional stake in how she did. Therefore I am proud to say that while I was writing this case study she called to tell me she had passed. In fact she plans to take another English course during the summer since she wants to improve her writing still more. At the end of the conversation, we wished each other a good vacation, and my tutoring experience ended—a happy one.

him to do it. Point out a couple misspelled words. Two odd sentences. Matt still doesn't talk too much. Very different than Adam who just keeps chattering away, even while he is working on something. Adam is working on one of those old fashioned business letter assignments. Write a letter applying for a job. Supposed to work on the student's writing-to-an-audience skills. Adam is clearly a remedial reader and writer. He spells some very simple words wrong. He always seems to be doing assignments right before they are due. And he is always trying to get me to do his work for him. And sometimes I relent and give him some answers.

Writing a Case Study

Another feature of the fifteen-week training course is to require students to compose an in-depth case study. This report may be a holistic discussion of their overall tutoring or it may zero in on the tutor's interaction over time with one writer. Students can draw from information in their journals to compile the case study. They might also want to attach copies of relevant documents (the writer's notes, drafts, revisions) that exemplify and dramatize the twists and turns, successes and failures that occurred during their tutoring tenure. The case study should pinpoint writing problems that the tutor identified, strategies recommended to the writer, and how (and if) the problems were resolved. Figure 11–8 is a case study that one of our students, Tom, submitted at the end of a tutor training course. It demonstrates how Tom reconstructed his semester-long work with one writer, a college freshman named Cynthia.

Record-Keeping Devices

In most tutorial programs, it is important to carefully document the number of tutorial sessions, keep track of who tutored whom, record what happened during each one-to-one meeting, and assess the quality of the tutoring. To prevent them from being swamped by unnecessary paperwork that might sidetrack them from the real business of tutoring, we present our tutoring students with some time-tested record-keeping forms that allow tutorial activity to be chronicled painlessly and accurately. Part of our training course involves convincing tutors to maintain these records diligently. Figure 11–4 shows the Writing Tutor Log Sheet, which tutors fill out and file immediately after a tutoring session. Figure 11–5 is a sample of an observation form filled out by the teacher/trainer after sitting in on a tutorial session, in order to evaluate the effectiveness of the writing tutor and to guide an assessment conference. Figure 11–6 approaches evaluation from the writer's perspective, by seeking her evaluation of how a given writing tutorial went.

Electronic Resources

OWLs

At Colleges and Universities

Purdue University Online Writing Lab
http://owl.english.purdue.edu

University of Missouri Online Writery
web.missouri.edu/~wleric/writery.html

Bowling Green State University Writing Lab
www.bgsu.edu/departments/writing-lab/index.html

Michigan Technological University Writing Center
www.hu.mtu.edu/wc

University of Maine Writing Center Online
www.ume.maine.edu/~wcenter/

University of Michigan Online Writing Lab
www.lsa.umich.edu/swc/OWL/owl.html

University of Oregon WORD (Writing Online Resource Directory)
www.uoregon.edu/~uocomp/word.html

At Two-year and Community Colleges

Roane State Community College Online Writing Lab
www.rscc.cc.tn.us/owl/owl.html

At Secondary Schools

Webb School OWL
gateway.webb.pvt.k12.tn.us/owl/webbowl.html

Software

Aspects Simultaneous Conference Software
Group Logic, Inc.
4350 North Fairfax Drive, Suite 900
Arlington, VA 22203

Daedalus Integrated Writing Environment
The Daedalus Group, Inc.
1106 Clayton Lane, #510W
Austin, TX 78723

MOOs and MUDs

CollegeTown

A virtual college community with coauthored and collaborative writing among students and students-faculty: www.bou.edu/ctown/webmooy.html

DaedalusMOO

A coauthoring and collaborative writing environment, part of the Daedalus Integrated Writing Environment software: www.daedalus.com/moo.html

Diversity University

An interactive learning virtual university with many coauthoring and collaborative possibilities: www.du.org

Lingua MOO

A community of rhetoric, writing, and humanities graduate students, faculty members, and researchers: http://lingua.utdallas.edu

Lost Library of MOO

Links to many sites with information about MOOs: www.hayseed.net/moo

Virtual Writing Center MOO

Tutoring, coauthoring, and writing courses: http://bessie.englab.slcc.edu/moo/connect

References

Allen, H. 1975. "A '60s Superhero After the Acid Test." In *Writing in Style,* edited by L. Babb. Boston: Houghton Mifflin.

Alvino, J. 1995. *Considerations and Strategies for Parenting the Gifted Child.* Storrs, CT: National Research Center for the Gifted and Talented.

Annis, L. F. 1983. The Processes and Effects of Peer Tutoring. Paper presented at the annual meeting of the American Educational Research Association, April, Montreal, Canada. ERIC Document Reproduction Service No. ED 228 964.

Atherley, C. A. 1989. "Shared Reading: An Experiment in Peer Tutoring in the Primary Classroom." *Educational Studies* 15 (2): 145–53.

Atwell, N., ed. 1990. *Coming to Know: Writing to Learn in the Intermediate Grades.* Portsmouth, NH: Heinemann.

———. 1998. *In the Middle: New Understandings About Writing, Reading, and Learning.* Portsmouth, NH: Heinemann.

Baghban, M. 1984. *Our Daughter Learns to Read and Write: A Case Study from Birth to Three.* Newark, DE: International Reading Association.

Bakhtin, M. M. 1981. "Discourse in the Novel." In *The Dialogic Imagination,* edited by M. Holquist; translated by C. Emerson and M. Holquist, 72–94. Austin, TX: University of Texas Press.

Barnes, D. 1990. "Oral Language and Learning." In *Perspectives on Talk and Learning,* edited by S. Hynds and D. L. Rubin, 41–54. Urbana, IL: National Council of Teachers of English.

Beaven, M. H. 1977. "Individualized Goal Setting, Self-Evaluation, and Peer Evaluation." In *Evaluating Writing: Describing, Measuring, Judging,* edited by C. R. Cooper and L. Odell. Urbana, IL: National Council of Teachers of English.

Belenky, M., B. Clinchy, N. Goldberger, and J. M. Tarule. 1986. *Women's Ways of Knowing: the Development of Self, Voice, and Mind.* New York: Basic Books.

Benard, B. 1990. *The Case for Peers.* Portland, OR: Northwest Regional Educational Laboratory. ERIC Document Reproduction Service No. ED 327 755.

Benesch, S. 1985. Improving Peer Response: Collaboration Between Teachers and Students. Paper presented at the annual meeting of the Conference on College Composition and Communication, March, New York. ERIC Document Reproduction Service No. ED 243 113.

Berg, A. S. 1978. *Max Perkins: Editor of Genius.* New York: Simon and Schuster.

Bishop, W. 1992. Writing from the Tips of Our Tongues: Writers, Tutors, and Talk. Paper presented at the annual Peer Tutoring in Writing Conference, October, Indiana, PA. ERIC Document Reproduction Service No. ED 350 629.

————, ed. 1997. *Elements of Alternate Style: Essays on Writing and Revision.* Portsmouth, NH: Heinemann.

Bleich, D. 1975. *Readings and Feelings: An Introduction to Subjective Criticism.* Urbana, IL: National Council of Teachers of English.

Bolton, F., and D. Snowball. 1993. *Ideas for Spelling.* Portsmouth, NH: Heinemann.

Bomer, R. 1995. *Time for Meaning.* Portsmouth, NH: Heinemann.

Brown, T. 1983. *Tom Brown's Field Guide to Nature Observation and Tracking.* New York: Berkley Books.

Bruffee, K. A. 1973. "Collaborative Learning: Some Practical Models." *College English* 34: 220–38.

————. 1978. "The Brooklyn Plan: Attaining Intellectual Growth Through Peer Group Tutoring." *Liberal Education* 64: 447–69.

————. 1980. "Staffing and Operating Peer-Tutoring Writing Centers." In *Basic Writing,* edited by L. Kasden and D. Hoeber, 141–49. Urbana, IL: National Council of Teachers of English.

————. 1986. "Social Construction, Language, and the Authority of Knowledge: A Bibliographic Essay." *College English* 48: 773–90.

Budz, J., and T. Grabar. 1976. "Tutorial Versus Classroom in Freshmen English." *College Composition and Communication* 37: 654–56.

Burke, K. 1945. *A Grammar of Motives.* Englewood Cliffs, NJ: Prentice-Hall.

Cairney, T. H., and L. Munsie. 1991. Talking to Literacy Learners: A Parent Education Project. Paper presented at the International Convention on Language and Literacy, April, Norwich, England.

Canadian Teachers Federation. 1991. *Literacy in the Classroom: Reports of Classroom Research Projects Conducted by Teachers.* Ottawa, ONT: Canadian Teachers Federation. ERIC Document Reproduction Service No. ED 335 670.

Carli, S. M. 1996. *Improving Reading Comprehension and Word Attack Skills Through Cross-Age Tutoring.* Chicago, IL: Loyola University. ERIC Document Reproduction Service No. ED 409 526.

Clark, B. L. 1985. *Talking About Writing: A Guide for Tutor and Teacher Conferences.* Ann Arbor, MI: University of Michigan Press.

Clark, I. L. 1985. *Writing in the Center: Teaching in a Writing Center Setting.* Dubuque, IA: Kendall/Hunt.

Clark, R., and D. Fry. 1992. *Coaching Writers: Editors and Reporters Working Together.* New York: St. Martin's Press.

Cohen, P. A., J. A. Kulik, and C-L. C. Kulik. 1982. "Educational Outcomes of

Peer Tutoring: A Meta-analysis of Findings." *American Educational Research Journal* 19: 237–48.

Cramer, S., and T. Reigstad. 1994. "Using Personality to Teach Writing." *Composition Chronicle* March: 4–7.

Cravens, J. 1997. "Clear Correct Writing Is Vital to All Businesses." *San Diego Business Journal* 18: 19–20.

Daly, J. A., and M. D. Miller. 1975. "The Empirical Development of an Instrument to Measure Writing Apprehension." *Research in the Teaching of English* 9: 242–49.

Danis, F. 1980. Peer Response Groups in a College Writing Workshop: Students' Suggestions for Revising Compositions. *Dissertation Abstracts International*, 41, 5008a–5009a. University Microfilms DA2319876.

Daro, P. 1993. *New Standards Project*. Oakland, CA: University of California.

David, D. L. 1985. "An Ethnographic Investigation in Small Group Writing Workshops in a College Writing Class." Buffalo, NY: SUNY/Buffalo. ERIC Document Reproduction Service No. ED 285 154.

Davis, K. 1987. Improving Students' Writing Attitudes: The Effects of the Writing Center. Paper presented at the annual meeting of the East Central Writing Center Association, May, Youngstown, OH. ERIC Document Reproduction Service No. ED 294 183.

Davis, K. W. 1995. "What Writing Training Can—and Can't—Do." *Training* 32: 60–63.

Davis, P. 1991. "Parents Writing with Students." *English Journal* 80: 62–64.

Delpit, L. 1988. "The Silenced Dialogue: Power and Pedagogy in Educating Other People's Children." *Harvard Educational Review* 58: 280–98.

Deming, M. P. 1986. Peer Tutoring and the Teaching of Writing. Paper presented at the annual meeting of the Southeastern Writing Center Association, April, Mobile, AL. ERIC Document Reproduction Service No. ED 276 019.

DiPardo, A., and S. W. Freedman. 1988. "Peer Response Groups in the Writing Classroom: Theoretic Foundations and New Directions." *Review of Educational Research* 58 (2): 119–49.

DiTiberio, J., and G. Jensen. 1994. *Writing and Personality: Finding Your Voice, Your Style, Your Way*. Palo Alto, CA: Davies-Black Publishing.

Doctorow, E. L. 1988. "E. L. Doctorow." In *Writers at Work*, edited by G. Plimpton. New York: Penguin.

Dowd, M. 1999. "Hunker in the Bunker." *The New York Times*, 25 April, 17.

Drechsel, J. 1989. "Peer Groups and the Language of Negotiation." *Working Papers in Educational Linguistics* 5 (2): 52–68. ERIC Document Reproduction Service No. ED 335 926.

Eakins, B. W., and R. G. Eakins. 1978. *Sex Differences in Human Communication*. Boston: Houghton Mifflin.

Elbow, P. 1973. *Writing Without Teachers.* New York: Oxford University Press.

———. 1981. *Writing with Power.* New York: Oxford University Press.

Emig, J. 1969. *The Composing Process of Twelfth Graders.* Urbana, IL: National Council of Teachers of English.

Florio-Ruane, S. 1986. Taking a Closer Look at Writing Conferences. Paper presented at the annual meeting of the American Educational Research Association, April, San Francisco, CA. ERIC Document Reproduction Service No. ED 275 003.

Flower, L. 1981. *Problem-Solving Strategies for Writing.* New York: Harcourt, Brace, and Jovanovich.

Flower, L., and J. R. Hayes. 1977. "Problem-Solving Strategies and the Writing Process." *College English* 39: 449–61.

———. 1981. "A Cognitive Process Theory of Writing." *College Composition and Communication* 35: 365–87.

Freedman S. W. 1980. Teaching and Learning in the Writing Conference. Paper presented at the annual meeting of the Conference on College Composition and Communication, March, San Francisco, CA. ERIC Document Reproduction Service No. ED 185 599.

———. 1981. "Evaluation in the Writing Conference: An Interactive Process." In *Selected Papers from the 1981 Texas Writing Research Conference,* edited by M. C. Hairston and C. L. Selfe, 65–96. Austin, TX: University of Texas at Austin.

———. 1987. *Peer Response Groups in Two Ninth-Grade Classrooms* (Technical Report No. 12). Berkeley, CA: Center for the Study of Writing, University of California, Berkeley.

Freedman S. W., and R. Calfee. 1984. "Understanding and Comprehending." *Written Communication* 1: 459–90.

Freedman, S. W., and M. Sperling. 1985. "Written Language Acquisition: The Role of Response and the Writing Conference." In *The Acquisition of Written Language: Response and Revision,* edited by S. W. Freedman, 106–30. Norwood, NJ: Ablex.

Freire, P., and F. Macedo. 1987. *Literacy: Reading the Word and the World.* South Hadley, MA: Bergin and Garvey.

Garcia Marquez, G. 1984. "Gabriel Garcia Marquez." In *Writers at Work,* edited by G. Plimpton. New York: Penguin.

Gardner, H. 1985. *Multiple Intelligences.* New York: Basic Books.

Garrison, R. 1974. "One-to-One: Tutorial Instruction in Freshman Composition." *New Directions for Community Colleges* 2: 55–84.

———. 1979a. Interview with Tom Reigstad. April. Portland, ME.

———. 1979b. Letter to Tom Reigstad. 11 April.

———. 1979c. Letter to Tom Reigstad. 24 October.

———. 1981a. Letter to Tom Reigstad. 6 August.

———. 1981b. *One-to-One: Making Writing Instruction Effective.* Instructor's manual to accompany R. Garrison's *How a Writer Works.* New York: Harper & Row.

———. 1985. *How a Writer Works.* New York: Harper and Row.

Gautrey, F. 1990. "Cross-Age Tutoring in Frankley." *Reading* 24 (1): 21–27.

Gentry, J. R. 1996. *My Kid Can't Spell! Understanding and Assisting Your Child's Literacy Development.* Portsmouth, NH: Heinemann.

George, D. 1984. "Writing with Peer Groups in Composition." *College Composition and Communication* 35: 320–36.

Gere, A. R. 1982. "Students' Oral Response to Written Composition." Seattle, WA: University of Washington. ERIC Document Reproduction Service No. ED 229 781.

———. 1987. *Writing Groups: History, Theory, and Implications.* Carbondale, IL: Southern Illinois University Press.

Gere, A. R., and R. D. Abbott. 1985. "Talking About Writing: The Language of Writing Groups." *Research in the Teaching of English* 19: 362–79.

Gibson, W. 1966. *Tough, Sweet and Stuffy: An Essay on Modern American Prose Styles.* Bloomington, IN: Indiana University Press.

———. 1969. *Persona: A Style Study for Readers and Writers.* New York: Random House.

———. 1979a. Interview with Tom Reigstad. April. Amherst, MA.

———. 1979b. "The Writing Teacher as a Dumb Reader." *College Composition and Communication* 30: 192–95.

Gilliam, A. M. 1990. "Research in the Classroom: Learning Through Response." *English Journal* 79: 98–99.

Gilligan, C. 1982. *In a Different Voice: Psychological Theory and Women's Development.* Cambridge, MA: Harvard University Press.

Ginsberg, A. 1996. "Is About." *The New Yorker* (21–28 October): 197.

Goldstein, L. M., and S. M. Conrad. 1990. "Student Input and Negotiation of Meaning in ESL Writing Conferences." *TESOL Quarterly* 24: 443–60.

Gorman, T. P. 1981. "A Survey of Attainment and Progress of Learners in Adult Literacy Schemes." *Educational Researcher* 23: 190–98.

Graves, D. 1983. *Writing: Teachers and Children at Work.* Exeter, NH: Heinemann.

———. 1991. *Build a Literate Classroom.* Portsmouth, NH: Heinemann.

———. 1994. *A Fresh Look at Writing.* Portsmouth, NH: Heinemann.

———. 1996. "If You Write, They Will Too." *Instructor* January/February: 40–41.

Greenwood, C. R., J. C. Delquadri, and R. V. Hall. 1989. "Longitudinal Effects of Classwide Peer Tutoring." *Journal of Educational Psychology* 81: 371–83.

Hacker, T. 1994. Teacher Conferences as a Modeling Technique for Peer

Response. Paper presented at the annual meeting of the Conference on College Composition and Communication, March, Nashville, TN. ERIC Document Reproduction Service No. ED 372 404.

Hahn, A. L., and T. Smith. 1983. "Students' Differentiation of Reader-Based and Text-Based Questions." *Journal of Educational Research* 76 (6): 331–34.

Hall, N. 1991. *Exploring Chaos: A Guide to the New Science of Disorder.* New York: W. W. Norton.

Hall, R. 1994. *The Effect of Cooperative Learning, Cross-Age Tutoring, and Self-Esteem Enhancing Strategies on Student Behavior and Reading Achievement.* Bloomington, IN: Indiana University. ERIC Document Reproduction Service No. ED 371 322.

Hamilton-Wieler, S. 1990. Collaborative Classrooms: Building a Community of Writers. Paper presented at the Indiana University Fall Language Conference, November, Bloomington, IN. ERIC Document Reproduction Service No. ED 324 679.

Haring-Smith, T. 1992. "Changing Students' Attitudes: Writing Fellows Program." In *Writing Across the Curriculum: A Guide to Developing Programs,* edited by S. H. McLeod and M. Soven, 175–188. Newbury Park, CA: Sage.

Harris, M. 1986. *Teaching One-to-One: The Writing Conference.* Urbana, IL: National Council of Teachers of English.

———. 1992. "The Writing Center and Tutoring in WAC Programs." In *Writing Across the Curriculum: A Guide to Developing Programs,* edited by S. H. McLeod and M. Soven, 155–174. Newbury Park, CA: Sage.

———. 1995. "Why Writers Need Writing Tutors." *College English* 57: 27–42.

Harris, M., and T. Silva. 1993. "Tutoring ESL Students: Issues and Options." *College Composition and Communication* 44: 525–37.

Harste, J. C., V. A. Woodward, and C. L. Burke. 1984. *Language Stories and Literacy Lessons.* Portsmouth, NH: Heinemann.

Hawkins, T. 1976. *Group Inquiry Techniques for Teaching Writing.* Urbana, IL: National Council of Teachers of English.

Heat-Moon, W. L. 1991. *Blue Highways.* Boston: Houghton Mifflin.

Hedin, D. 1987. "Students as Teachers: A Tool for Improving School Climate and Productivity." *Social Policy* 17 (3): 42–47.

Herrscher, W. 1985. "The Joy of Titles: Christening Your Composition." *Teaching English in the Two-Year College* December: 287–291.

Hersh, S. 1993. "On the Nuclear Edge." *The New Yorker* (29 March): 56–73.

Hoffman, G., and G. Hoffman. 1997. *Adios, Strunk and White.* Huntington Beach, CA: Verve Press.

Hooper, R. 1993. "Breaking the Waiting List Logjam: Training Peer Tutors for ESL." In *Reflections: An Anthology of Selections from the "All Write News," the Newsletter of the Adult Literacy Resource Institute,* edited by S. Reuys, 35–45. Boston: Adult Literacy Resource Institute. ERIC Document Reproduction Service No. ED 373 265.

Hubbuch, S. 1988. "A Tutor Needs to Know the Subject Matter to Help a Student Write a Paper: ___Agree ___Disagree ___Not Sure." *Writing Center Journal* 8 (2): 23–30.

Hunzer, K. M. 1994. Gender Expectations and Relationships in the Writing Center. Paper presented at the annual meeting of the Conference on College Composition and Communication, March, Nashville, TN.

Jacobs, S., and A. Karliner. 1977. "Helping Writers to Think: The Effect of Speech Roles in Individual Conferences on the Quality of Thought in Student Writing." *College English* 38: 489–505.

Johns, A. M. 1995. "Genre and Pedagogical Purposes." *Journal of Second Language Writing* 4: 181–90.

Joos, M. 1961. *The Five Clocks.* New York: Harcourt Brace.

Jordan-Henley, J., and B. M. Maid. 1995. "Tutoring in Cyberspace: Student Impact and College/University Collaboration." *Computers and Composition* 12: 211–18.

Judy, J. E., P. A. Alexander, J. M. Kulikowich, and V. L. Willson. 1988. "Effects of Two Instructional Approaches and Peer Tutoring on Gifted and Nongifted Sixth-Grade Students' Analogy Performance." *Reading Research Quarterly* 23 (2): 236–56.

Kates, J. 1977. *Individual Conferences Versus Typed Comments Without Conferences on Graded Freshmen English Composition Papers: The El Camino Experiment and the Compton Experiment.* ERIC Document Reproduction Service No. ED 140 910.

Kiedaisch, J., and S. Dinitz. 1991. "Learning More from Students." *The Writing Center Journal* 12: 90–100.

———. 1993. "Look Back and Say 'So What': the Limitations of the Generalist Tutor." *Writing Center Journal* 14 (1): 63–74

Kinkead, J. 1985. Tutors in the Writing Center. Paper presented at the annual meeting of the Conference on College Composition and Communication, March, Minneapolis, MN.

Klinkenborg, V. 1992. Talk at Buffalo State College, Buffalo, NY, 20 February.

Kosko, B. 1993. *Fuzzy Thinking: The New Science of Fuzzy Logic.* New York: Hyperion.

Kroeger, L. 1993. "Coaching the Internal Audit Team to Success." *Internal Auditor* 50: 59–62.

Kurth, L. 1995. Democracy and Leadership in Basic Writing Small Groups. Paper presented at the annual meeting of the Conference on College Composition and Communication, March, Washington, DC. ERIC Document Reproduction Service No. ED 384 871.

Lagana, J. R. 1972. The Development, Implementation, and Evaluation of a Model for Teaching Composition Which Utilizes Individualized Learning and Peer Grouping. *Dissertation Abstracts International,* 73, 04127a, University Microfilms DA5639276.

Land, W. 1987. *Effects of Peer Tutoring in Middle School English Classes.* Mississippi State University Bureau of Educational Research and Evaluation. ERIC Document Reproduction Service No. ED 290 143.

Leach, M. P. 1987. Effectiveness of a Language Arts Tutoring Program as Perceived by the Elementary Students. Paper presented at the annual meeting of the Mid-South Educational Research Association, November, Mobile, AL. ERIC Document Reproduction Service No. ED 345 142.

Levin, H. M., G. V. Glass, and G. R. Meister. 1984. *The Cost Effectiveness of Four Educational Interventions.* Stanford, CA: Stanford University, Institute for Educational Finance and Governance. ERIC Document Reproduction Service No. ED 246 533.

Lindfors, J. W. 1985. "Oral Language Learning: Understanding the Development of Language Structure." In *Observing the Language Learner,* edited by A. Jaggar and M. T. Smith-Burke. Urbana, IL: National Council of Teachers of English and International Reading Association.

Lines, P. M. 1997. *Homeschooling: An Overview for Educational Policymakers.* January. Washington, DC: U.S. Department of Education Working Paper.

Lunsford, A. A., and L. Ede. 1986. Collaboration in Writing on the Job: A Research Report. Paper presented at the annual meeting of the Conference on College Composition and Communication, March, New Orleans, LA. ERIC Document Reproduction Service No. ED 268 582.

MacDonald, R. B. 1987. Evaluation of an Alternative Solution for the Assessment and Retention of High-Risk College Students. Paper presented at the annual meeting of the American Educational Research Association, April, Washington, DC. ERIC Document Reproduction Service No. ED 316 302.

Macrorie, K. 1970. *Telling Writing.* Rochelle Park, NJ: Hayden.

Maher, F. A., and M. K. Thompson Tetreault. 1994. *The Feminist Classroom.* New York: Basic Books.

Martino, L. R. 1994. "Peer Tutoring for Young Adolescents, a Cost Effective Strategy." *Middle School Journal* 18 (2): 55–58.

Mavrogenes, N. A. 1990. "Helping Parents Help Their Children Become Literate." *Young Children* 45: 4–9.

McCleary, B. 1988. "UNH's Apostle of Conferencing and the Process Approach Retires from Teaching." *Composition Chronicle* 1 (February): 1–2.

———. 1998. "Schools Cannot Solve All Problems with Low Levels of Literacy." *Composition Chronicle* 11 (2): 1–4.

McCourt, F. 1996. *Angela's Ashes.* New York: Scribner.

McManus, G., and D. Kirby. 1988. "Research in the Classroom: Using Peer Group Instruction to Teach Writing." *English Journal* 77 (3): 78–79.

McPhee, J. 1976. *Coming into the Country.* New York: Farrar, Straus, and Giroux.

Meroney, B. 1994. *Improving the Literacy Growth of Second Grade Students*

Through the Use of Whole Language, Peer Tutoring, Cooperative Learning, and Computer-Based Instruction. Miami, FL: Nova University. ERIC Document Reproduction Service No. ED 376 442.

Meyer, E., and L. Z. Smith. 1987. *The Practical Tutor.* New York: Oxford University Press.

Meyer, S. 1988. "Prose by Any Other Name: A Context for Teaching the Rhetoric of Titles." *Journal of Advanced Composition* 8: 71–81.

Miles, M. B., and A. M. Huberman. 1984. *Qualitative Data Analysis: A Sourcebook of New Methods.* Beverly Hills, CA: Sage.

Moffett, J. 1985. "Hidden Impediments." In *Language, Schooling and Society,* edited by S. Tchudi, 89–100. Upper Montclair, NJ: Boynton/Cook.

Mooney, C. 1986. *The Effects of Peer Tutoring on Student Achievement.* Elizabeth, NJ: Kean College. ERIC Document Reproduction Service No. ED 270 739.

Moran, C. 1994. "How the Writing Process Came to UMass/Amherst: Roger Garrison, Donald Murray, and Institutional Change." In *Taking Stock: The Writing Process Movement in the '90s,* edited by L. Tobin and T. Newkirk, 133–152. Portsmouth, NH: Heinemann.

Morgan, R. P. 1990. *Tutoring: A Description of an Ongoing Research Program.* Chicago: University of Illinois. ERIC Document Reproduction Service No. ED 314 458.

Morrow, D. S. 1991. "Tutoring Writing: Healing or What?" *College Composition and Communication* 42: 218–29.

Murphy, C. 1989. "Freud in the Writing Center: The Psychoanalytics of Tutoring Well." *The Writing Center Journal* 10: 13–18.

Murray, D. 1961. "How to Get Started as a Free-Lance Writer." In *Prose by Professionals,* edited by T. Morris, 19–24. Garden City, NY: Doubleday.

———. 1979a. Interview with Tom Reigstad. April. Durham, NH.

———. 1979b. "The Listening Eye: Reflections on the Writing Conference." *College English* 41 (September): 13–18.

———. 1982a. *Learning by Teaching: Selected Articles on Writing and Teaching.* Montclair, NJ: Boynton/Cook.

———. 1982b. "Teaching the Other Self: The Writer's First Reader." *College Composition and Communication* 33 (May): 140–147.

———. 1983. *Writing for Your Readers.* Chester, CT: Globe Pequoit Press.

———. 1984. *Writing to Learn.* New York: Holt, Rinehart and Winston.

———. 1985. *A Writing Teacher Teaches Writing.* Boston: Houghton Mifflin.

———. 1989. *Expecting the Unexpected.* Portsmouth, NH: Heinemann.

———. 1995. *The Craft of Revision.* New York: Harcourt Brace.

Myers, I. B., and M. H. McCaulley. 1985. *Manual: A Guide to the Development and Use of the Myers Briggs Type Indicator.* Palo Alto, CA: Consulting Psychologists Press.

Newkirk, T. 1979a. Interview with Tom Reigstad. April. Durham, NH.

———. 1979b. "Read the Papers in Class." In *How to Handle the Paper Load,* edited by G. Stanford. Urbana, IL: National Council of Teachers of English.

———. 1989. "The First Five Minutes: Setting the Agenda in a Writing Conference." In *Writing and Response: Theory, Practice, and Research,* edited by C. Anson, 317–331. Urbana, IL: National Council of Teachers of English.

———. 1995. "The Writing Conference as Performance." *Research in the Teaching of English* 29: 193–215.

Noguchi, R. 1991. *Grammar and the Teaching of Writing: Limits and Possibilities.* Urbana, IL: National Council of Teachers of English.

Okawa, G., T. Fox, L. J. Y. Chang, S. R. Windsor, F. B. Chavez Jr., and L. Hayes. 1991. "Multi-Cultural Voices: Peer Tutoring and Critical Reflection in the Writing Center." *The Writing Center Journal* 12: 11–32.

Patthey-Chavez, G. G., and D. R. Ferris. 1997. "Writing Conferences and the Weaving of Multi-Voiced Texts in College Composition." *Research in the Teaching of English* 31: 51–90.

Perl, S. 1978. "The Composing Processes of Unskilled College Writers." *Research in the Teaching of English* 13: 317–36.

Perry, M. J. 1991. *The Effects of a Peer Tutoring Intervention Program on the Reading Levels of Underachieving Fifth-Grade Students.* Miami, FL: Nova University. ERIC Document Reproduction Service No. ED 333 360.

Pickens, J., and S. McNaughton. 1988. "Peer Tutoring of Comprehension Strategies." *Educational Psychology* 8 (1): 67–80.

Powers, J. K. 1993. "Rethinking Writing Center Conferencing Strategies for the ESL Writer." *The Writing Center Journal* 13: 29–47.

Pynchon, T. 1997. *Mason and Dixon.* New York: Henry Holt and Co.

Reid, J. 1994. "Responding to ESL Students Texts: The Myths of Appropriation." *TESOL Quarterly* 28: 273–92.

Reigstad, M. 1990. The Teacher as Editor: What Not to Emulate. Unpublished manuscript.

Reigstad, T. 1979. Follow-up Questionnaire with Laura. November.

———. 1980. Conferencing Practices of Professional Writers: Ten Case Studies. Unpublished dissertation, Buffalo, New York.

Reigstad, T., and D. A. McAndrew. 1984. *Training Tutors for Writing Conferences.* Urbana, IL: National Council of Teachers of English.

Rekrut, M. D. 1994. "Peer and Cross-Age Tutoring: The Lessons from Research." *Journal of Reading* 37: 356–62.

Rief, L. 1992. *Seeking Diversity.* Portsmouth, NH: Heinemann.

Rizzo, B. 1975. "Peer Teaching in English I." *College Composition and Communication* 26: 395–99.

Rogers, C. 1951. *Client-Centered Therapy.* Boston: Houghton Mifflin.

Romano, T. 1987. *Clearing the Way: Working with Teenage Writers*. Portsmouth, NH: Heinemann.

———. 1988. "Breaking the Rules in Style." *English Journal* 77 (8): 58–62.

———. 1995. *Writing with Passion: Life Stories, Multiple Genres*. Portsmouth, NH: Heinemann.

Rose, M. 1984. *Writer's Block: The Cognitive Dimension*. Carbondale, IL: Southern Illinois University Press.

Rosenblatt, L. M. 1978. *The Reader, the Text, and the Poem: The Transactional Theory of the Literary Work*. Carbondale, IL: Southern Illinois University Press.

Ross, S. F. 1972. *A Study to Determine the Effects of Peer Tutoring on the Reading Efficiency and Self Concept of Disadvantaged Community College Freshmen: Final Report*. Fort Worth, TX: Tarrant County Junior College District. ERIC Document Reproduction Service No. ED 081 415.

Rubin, D. L., and W. M. Dodd. 1987. *Talking into Writing*. Urbana, IL: National Council of Teachers of English.

Scanlan, C. 1983. *How I Wrote the Story: A Book for Writers by Writers About Writing*. Providence, RI: Providence Journal Company.

Scanlon, L. 1986. "Recruiting and Training Tutors for Cross-Disciplinary Writing Programs." *Writing Center Journal* 6 (1): 37–42.

Scardamalia, M., and C. Bereiter. 1985. "Written Composition." In *Handbook of Research on Teaching*, 3d ed., edited by M. Wittrock, 424–473. Skokie, IL: Rand McNally.

Shannon, R. F. Jr. 1983. A Small Group, Personal Growth Method for the Teaching of Writing. *Dissertation Abstracts International*, 44, 1714A. University Microfilms DA8324128.

Shaughnessy, M. 1977. *Errors and Expectations*. New York: Oxford University Press.

Simmons, J. 1979. *Report on the Experiment Testing the Effectiveness of the One-to-One Method of Teaching Composition*. Los Angeles: Los Angeles Community College District Office of Educational Programs.

Slavin, R. E. 1991. *Student Team Learning: A Practical Guide to Cooperative Learning*. Washington, DC: National Education Association. ERIC Document Reproduction Service No. ED 339 518.

Smith, C. B. 1993. *Parents as Tutors in Reading and Writing*. (Learning Package No. 51). Bloomington, IN: Indiana University, Smith Research Center. ERIC Document Reproduction Service No. ED 379 589.

Smith, F. 1988. *Joining the Literacy Club: Further Essays into Education*. Portsmouth, NH: Heinemann.

Smith, L., and G. Smith. 1988. "A Multivariate Analysis of Remediation Efforts with Developmental Students." *Teaching English in the Two-Year College* 15: 45–52.

Smith, L. Z. 1986. "Independence and Collaboration: Why We Should Decentralize Writing Centers." *Writing Center Journal* 7 (1): 3–10.

Smith, M. E. 1975. *Peer Tutoring in a Writing Workshop*. (Doctoral Dissertation, University of Michigan.) *Dissertation Abstracts International, 35,* 3623A.

Soliday, M. 1995. "Shifting Roles in Classroom Tutoring: Cultivating the Art of Boundary Crossing." *Writing Center Journal* 16 (1): 59–73.

Sommers, E. 1994. Peer Groups in Evolution: Inventing Classroom Communities. Paper presented at the annual meeting of the Conference on College Composition and Communication, March, Cincinnati, OH. ERIC Document Reproduction Service No. ED 345 290.

Sommers, N. 1982. "Responding to Student Writing." *College Composition and Communication* 33: 148–56.

Song, B., and E. Richter. 1997. "Tutoring in the Classroom: A Quantitative Study." *Writing Center Journal* 18: 50–60.

Sperling, M. 1990. "I Want to Talk to Each of You: Collaboration and the Teacher-Student Writing Conference." *Research in the Teaching of English* 24: 279–321.

———. 1991. "Dialogues of Deliberation: Conversations in the Teacher-Student Writing Conference." *Written Communication* 8: 131–62.

Sutton, D. G. 1975. Evaluating Teaching Methods in Composition. Paper presented at the annual meeting of the Conference on College Composition and Communication, March, St. Louis, MO. ERIC Document Reproduction Service No. ED 120 730.

Tannen, D. 1990. *You Just Don't Understand: Women and Men in Conversation* New York: William Morrow.

Taylor, D. 1983. *Family Literacy: Young Children Learning to Read and Write*. London: Heinemann.

Thames, D. G., and C. K. Reeves. 1994. "Poor Readers' Attitudes: Effects of Using Interests and Trade Books in an Integrated Language Arts Approach." *Reading Research and Instruction* 33: 293–308.

Thompson, T. 1994. "Personality Preferences, Tutoring Styles, and Implications for Tutor Training." *The Writing Center Journal* 14: 137–49.

Thonus, T. 1993. "Tutors as Teachers: Assisting ESL/EFL Students in the Writing Center." *The Writing Center Journal* 13: 13–25.

Tomlinson, B. 1975. A Study of the Effectiveness of Individualized Writing Lab Instruction for Students in Remedial Freshmen Composition. Paper presented at the annual meeting of the Western College Reading Association, March, Anaheim, CA. ERIC Document Reproduction Service No. ED 108 241.

Toth, G. M. 1997. *The Effects of Cross-Age Peer Tutoring on the Writing Achievement of Sixth- and First-Grade Students*. Elizabeth, NJ: Kean College. ERIC Document Reproduction Service No. ED 405 593.

Trimbur, J. 1983. "Students or Staff: Thoughts on the Use of Peer Tutors in Writing Centers." *Writing Program Administration* 7: 33–38.

Tucker, A. 1990. "The Effects of Peer Tutoring on Writing Improvement in a Combined Kindergarten–First Grade Class." Norfolk, VA: Norfolk State College. ERIC Document Reproduction Service No. ED 331 071.

Ulichny, P., and K. A. Watson-Gegeo. 1989. "Interactions and Authority: The Dominant Interpretive Framework in Writing Conferences." *Discourse Processes* 12: 309–28.

Vygotsky, L. 1978. *Mind in Society: The Development of Higher Psychological Processes.* Cambridge, MA: Harvard University Press.

Waldrop, M. M. 1992. *Complexity: The Emerging Science at the Edge of Order and Chaos.* New York: Touchstone.

Walker, C. P., and D. Elias. 1987. "Writing Conferences Talk: Factors Associated with High- and Low-Rated Writing Conferences." *Research in the Teaching of English* 21: 266–85.

Wasik, B. A., and R. E. Slavin. 1993. "Preventing Early Reading Failure with One-to-One Tutoring: A Review of Five Programs." *Reading Research Quarterly* 28: 178–200.

Weathers, W. 1980. *An Alternate Style: Options in Composition.* Upper Montclair, NJ: Boynton/Cook.

Wells, G. 1986. *The Meaning Makers.* Portsmouth, NH: Heinemann.

Wiggins, G. 1993. Authentic Assessment: Focusing on Quality Outcomes. Talk at Suny College at Brockport. 22 October.

Wood, J. T. 1994. *Gendered Lives: Communication, Gender, and Culture.* Belmont, NY: Wadsworth.

Young, R., A. Becker, and K. Pike. 1970. *Rhetoric: Discovery and Change.* New York: Harcourt, Brace and World.

Zhu, W. 1995. "Effects of Training for Peer Response on Students' Comments and Interactions." *Written Communication* 12: 492–528.

Ziv, N. D. 1983. Peer Groups in the Composition Classroom: A Case Study. Paper presented at the annual meeting of the Conference on College Composition and Communication, March, Detroit, MI. ERIC Document Reproduction Service No. ED 229 799.

Zoellner, R. 1969. "Talk-Write: A Behavioral Pedagogy for Composition." *College English* 30: 267–320.